THE DON'T SWEAT GUIDE
FOR DADS

Other books by the editors of Don't Sweat Press

The Don't Sweat Affirmations

The Don't Sweat Guide for Couples

The Don't Sweat Guide for Graduates

The Don't Sweat Guide for Grandparents

The Don't Sweat Guide for Parents

The Don't Sweat Guide for Moms

The Don't Sweat Guide for Weddings

The Don't Sweat Guide to Golf

The Don't Sweat Stories

The Don't Sweat Guide to Travel

The Don't Sweat Guide to Weight Loss

The Don't Sweat Guide to Taxes

The Don't Sweat Guide to Retirement

The Don't Sweat Guide for Teachers

The Don't Sweat Guide for Newlyweds

THE DON'T SWEAT GUIDE
FOR DADS

Stopping Stress from Getting
in the Way of What Really Matters

By the Editors of Don't Sweat Press
Foreword by Richard Carlson, Ph.D.,
author of the bestselling *Don't Sweat the Small Stuff*

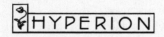

New York

Contents

Foreword

Someone recently asked me what I felt was the most important thing I had ever done in my life. It was the easiest question I've ever been asked. "Being a dad," I said, without even having to think about it. I didn't mention it at the time, but being a dad is also the toughest job I've ever had, and the most rewarding, by far.

Dads play a critical role in raising their kids. It's often said that "You can't replace a mom," and that's certainly true. But it's also true that you can't replace a dad. Dads have a special type of love for their kids that only we can offer. Dads also have a unique role to play, and many gifts to share. The pride and responsibility we feel toward our kids is truly extraordinary.

The editors of Don't Sweat Press have written what I believe is a very special guide for dads. As I've said, being a dad is a tough job, and every dad I've ever met wants to be the best dad he can be. Furthermore, every dad experiences at least some stress as a result of this important job.

I believe this book can help. It's full of great ideas to make the job of parenting even more fun and effective. There are also many good ideas to take some of the inevitable stress out of the job; ideas designed to help us keep our perspective. As I read through the book, I found myself saying, "Yes, that would be helpful."

To me, the most important insight about surviving the job of parenting in one piece is to realize that at least some of the stress we experience is self-generated. In other words, there are times when we use our own thinking against ourselves. We get too uptight and lose our bearings. We blow certain things out of proportion, and, when we do, we miss out on some of the best parts of the journey. This book helps us with some of that self-created stress!

Thank you for being the best dad you know how to be. Thank you also for reading books such as this one, designed to help us grow as dads, and to become even more loving, patient, and wise. I hope this book is of tremendous service to you, as it has been to me.

Treasure the gift of being a dad!
Richard Carlson
Benicia, California, 2003

THE DON'T SWEAT GUIDE
FOR DADS

1.

Remember That These
Are the Days

These days, most of us know all about the various stages of life, and we are encouraged to do a lot of thinking and planning ahead. Sometimes, though, we get so caught up in looking ahead that we miss the moments we are actually living in. We long for the weekend, count the days until vacation, and eagerly await the end of our children's infancy, toddler years, and adolescence. "If we can just get through this part," we think, "things will be so much better."

Your children only go through their childhoods once. They are helpless, demanding infants for a matter of months. Within a couple of years, they're on two feet and developing a fine, strong will of their own. Before you know it, they're spending as much or more time away as they are at home. As they increasingly choose the company of their peers, you cease to be the center of their universe. Before long, they begin to doubt your intelligence and resent your input in their lives. And then, one day, they're gone for weeks at a stretch, forgetting to call home, busy figuring out who they want to be.

All of this is natural. It's the way it's supposed to be. But each step forward for your children takes them closer to a life apart from you. If you don't live in and love the time you have under one roof with your kids, you forever miss one of the richest experiences life offers.

How do you make the most of your family life? First, keep your sense of humor well-tuned. Children are natural comedians. They see everything with fresh, curious eyes, and have the ability to be delighted by the tiniest surprises. Tune in to what they are doing and how they respond. Have a smile and a chuckle handy.

Keep your sense of balance in place, as well. You're the adult in the mix. Remember to look at both positive and negative events with perspective and patience.

Remember to exercise compassion. Growing up includes equal parts of joy and pain. Keep the memories of your experiences fresh in your mind and view your children's thoughts and actions through that lens.

Enjoying the challenges and pleasures of your child-rearing years takes balance, humor, and compassion. But even more, it requires that you be where you are, not always waiting for one thing to end or the next to start. Enjoy your children now. These are the days, and they won't come again.

2.

Choose Your Names Carefully

Our names are a daily part of our lives. What we are named at birth, and the nicknames and pet names we pick up along the way, can have a lifelong impact on us. So, too, for our children. Children take in and process aspects of their names in ways adults cannot realize. A name may seem like a small matter to you, but it can take on large proportions for your child.

Many new parents select a name for the quality it is said to describe—beauty, laughter, courage, or some other aspect of character. The name gives their child a positive quality to live up to. Parents may also teach their child to honor the family surname, because with that name, the child bears the family's reputation and respect. Similarly, parents may name their child after someone loved or esteemed. Here again, the sense that the child bears a name to be respected and upheld carries an import that can be taught and valued.

But those other names—nicknames chosen for fun, convenience, or saying "I love you"—can have impact, as well. Ask Bucky how

17

badly he wished his parents would get braces for his teeth. Ask Carrots how long it took her to start coloring her hair when she went to college. The point is that the informal names we give children have at least as much power—and sometimes more—to affect their views of themselves as their given names do.

Pay attention to the names and nicknames that you choose. Never use a name to exaggerate traits that can make a child self-conscious or self-deprecating. Steer clear of nicknames that will embarrass them in front of their friends, siblings, and others.

Nicknames and terms of endearment can be part of creating a special bond of closeness and connection between father and child, but they need to be chosen with the realization of their power. You figure greatly in your children's self-esteem, and the names you choose are an avenue to encourage and care for their fragile egos.

3.

Let Rank Have Its Privileges

Nobody enjoys being the bad guy. When you say no to something your children want and stand your ground, or when you insist on behavior your kids would prefer to avoid, you wear the bad-guy hat for a while. It's more fun to be a pal and be the one that they call "cool." But part of the dad business involves hard lines and insistence on certain things.

Children need boundaries, and they need to know what those boundaries are. When you give them a clear sense of what's okay and what's not, you give them much-needed guidance and a remarkable sense of being loved and protected, no matter what they may say to the contrary. They lack the experience and wisdom necessary to make many of the judgments and decisions that comprise their daily lives. Often, they also lack the power to handle the consequences of their own bad choices and misguided judgments. Don't doubt for a moment how much they need for you to be in charge.

With that in mind, consider a few caveats. First, exercising the authority of your position in your kids' lives does not preclude friendship. In fact, when you take your role as Dad seriously and act as the authority figure that you are, you offer the best kind of friendship. Just because you are the one in charge doesn't mean for a minute that you can't have fun with your kids, nor does it take away from your expressions of love.

Second, exercising your authority does not mean bullying. Nothing will undermine you faster as a dad than cavalierly controlling your children's lives or taking charge in a bad-tempered or pugnacious manner. Your children know the difference between loving rules and bullheadedness. Pull rank only when it's really needed, and over time, you'll earn your children's sincere respect.

Finally, exercising authority needs to grow and change with your children. The older that they get and the more that they know, the more you need to let them take responsibility for their choices—and yes, suffer some consequences. By doing so, you groom them for their futures as adults.

In all likelihood, your kids don't need more pals. They *do* need a dad who is a true friend and fills a dad's shoes.

4.

Accept Yourself

In this day and age, we receive multiple messages through the media, medical experts, and self-help experts that just about anything we don't like about ourselves can be changed. Join a gym, take up meditation, go into therapy, opt for corrective surgery—one way or another, whatever is bothering us can be fixed.

In truth, however, while some "fixes" are certainly within our reach and worth our attention, others may require extremes of resources or levels of resolve that are simply beyond us. Furthermore, some desired changes have more to do with the myths perpetuated by our culture than with reality.

It's important to realize that your children receive the same unhealthy messages about perfection that you do. They, too, are encouraged to believe that people can have the "perfect" look and demeanor, the "best" talents and aptitudes, or the "in" traits.

You can telegraph a counter-message that your children sorely need if they're going to build a healthy perspective on their own bodies and personality traits. You have it in your power to offer your children two of the most potent antidotes there are to the body and personality myths of our day.

First of all, your reaction to the way you yourself are made—particularly your ability to accept yourself for who and what you are intrinsically—will demonstrate the fact that human differences are not only a fact of life, but one of its fascinations. Before you criticize yourself for some perceived flaw, consider what you're teaching your kids about the relative importance of the givens in their basic makeup. They need a positive example of self-acceptance in their lives.

Beyond that, when you hear them taking a hypercritical view of themselves, be ready to step in with a hug and an unwavering expression of love and appreciation for who and what *they* are. They need to hear and feel from you that the way they are put together is one of life's great miracles, and one of your deepest joys. Your unchanging affirmation, day after day, year after year, offers them the solid ground of self-esteem to build on.

5.

Allow Secrets, Keep Secrets

One day, your child is a fountain of information about all that he or she is doing, learning, exploring, and experiencing. The next day, the fountain seems to be drying up. A simple question—"What happened in school today?"—that would previously have been answered in detail and with enthusiasm elicits only, "Nothing."

We all have secrets. It's part of being an individual. That's no less true for children than it is for adults. In fact, keeping secrets is one of the early steps in a child's separation from parents. It's one of the few ways that a child can say, "Some things are my business alone, because I am me, not you."

It's natural to feel a loss, and perhaps some alarm, when the secrets begin. But unless you have evidence that there's something to worry about—such as a change in personality, a new level of fears, or unexplained injuries—your wisest course is to let the secrets lie. Your children have a developmental need to pull away from you as they mature. It's your job to equip them to do so with all of the information that they need, and age-appropriate boundaries firmly in place. If you do your part and make yourself a strong presence in your children's lives, you need not concern yourself when you realize that they choose not to share everything.

On the other hand, you may sometimes be the person in whom your children decide to confide. Just as surely as you need to allow your kids to have secrets, you must be a worthy confidant. At times, kids' secrets are unbearably delicious, and you want to share them with other adults who will see the humor or innocence in the same way that you do. Resist that temptation. Too often, kids overhear their parents discussing the kids' personal lives with friends. When they do, they learn the unhappy lesson that their parents can't be trusted with a confidence.

In the same way, take care not to turn privileged information into fuel for teasing. It may win you a laugh from others, but it will lose a precious part of your relationship with your children. Treat your children the way you want to be treated. Honor their privacy and guard their secrets. You will be rewarded with their trust.

6.
Talk Straight

You're with your child. You make a playful crack. You get the look, the rolling eyes. You hear the semiexasperated, "Da-aad," accompanied by a groan. You've teased for the umpteenth time, and once again, you've scored.

For many fathers, teasing is a way of expressing love and affection to their children. They find it difficult to be more straightforward, and their children soon learn that teasing accompanied by a twinkle in the eye really means "I love you." Often, their response is their way of saying, "I love you, too."

But teasing can easily become sarcasm. At each stage of their lives, your children will act, think, or present themselves in ways that you disapprove of. The temptation to batter them with sarcasm in the name of teasing can be overwhelming. Sarcasm can be very effective, and even devastating, because it belittles; it comes with a barb attached. Instead of saying, "I love you," sarcasm says, "You're not my equal," or "You're not worthy."

Learn to speak from the mind and the heart, not from the hip. Verbal art is not what your children need from you. They need words without ambiguity or destructive overtones; they need words that heal and reveal. When you're tempted to make the quick quip, restrain yourself. Remind yourself of the precious charge before you and ask, "How can I best respond to this act or assertion?" Let your children learn about sarcasm somewhere else, and be the one who teaches them how to put it in its place.

7.

Respect as You
Want to Be Respected

What kind of feedback from others do you need in order to know that you're esteemed and valued? A pat on the back when you complete a project? Attentive silence when you're voicing your opinion? Some deference when an important decision needs to be made? Praise when you do something well? Recognition when you do something worthy? All of these responses tell us that we are respected. We understand that we are valued in a relationship, a job, or a community when others respond in these ways. We feel affirmed and encouraged.

Every human being deserves a fundamental level of respect. This includes a respect for life itself, for the value of every individual, and for each person's potential. While our children are young and living with us, we often notice all that needs to mature and grow. We become anxious about aspects that we don't admire in them, and eager to shape them according to our own ideals. But from the moment that they begin to exist, our children deserve the fundamental respect due to everyone. They tend to thrive when they receive it.

Children learn that they're respected through the same feedback that you do. Make a point of understanding the ways in which you want to receive respect, and consider how you can show such affirmation to your children. Pay attention to the character traits that they are developing, and give them positive reinforcement. Take note of their good efforts at home and in school, and praise them not only for achievements, but also for good efforts. Take their ideas and their gifts seriously, letting them know that who and what they are matters to you, and sometimes even impresses you. Assume that there may be occasions when *they're* right instead of you, and be prepared to say so. Ask their opinions and listen as though they can teach you something. In the context of your support and respect, they just might!

8.

Apologize Freely

Arguably, one of the worst lines ever written into a movie script asserted that love means never having to say you're sorry. Apologies are most important in a loving relationship. Yet dads too often feel that apologizing somehow diminishes a child's respect or lessens the sense of the dad's authority. Nothing could be further from the truth.

Kids have a strong, natural sense of what is honest and fair. Although they put on a good act when they aren't getting what they want from you, they often know that your decisions and rules are not unfair—just unappealing and aggravating at the time. Sometimes, however, you do or say the wrong thing—after all, we all make mistakes. You betray a confidence, act inappropriately out of anger, or misjudge your children. You hurt their feelings or cause them to miss an important event. You forget a promise or change the rules unexpectedly. An apology is in order, and that fact is not lost on your children.

You may find it hard to say "I'm sorry," even when you really feel sorry for your words or behavior. You have to get over it. Find a quiet moment when your child will hear you, and show how it's done—with meaning. Your ability to take responsibility for the times that you're in the wrong will teach your children more than all of the moral lectures you can spout. They'll see firsthand that admitting your faults and failures does not make you look smaller in the eyes of others. Rather, it shows you to be a person of character, depth, and humility. They'll understand that everyone makes mistakes, and they'll be better able to admit their own mistakes, learn from them, and move on.

Most important, when you apologize, you will build a foundation of honesty and respect in your relationship with your children. You may not enjoy the full benefits of this while the kids are still immature and wrestling their way into adulthood, but you will later, when you become their valued friend. All along the way, you'll have the satisfaction of giving them the best of yourself.

9.

Get Grubby

You may find it easy to settle down with the newspaper when you get home from work. You may prefer to spend your weekends and vacations in adult activities and home projects. Your kids will survive if you never make a mud pie or throw a ball. They'll live to tell the tale if you never wrestle, tickle, or act like a pony for their cowboy imitation. But they won't remember you as the heart of some of their happiest childhood memories; and you will have missed some of the most precious and spontaneous moments that occur between father and child.

Letting yourself be your children's playmate doesn't mean that you stop being the adult. It simply means that you let your children have access to your humor and sense of fun. You don't have to involve yourself in all of their games and play. You can pick the ones that you enjoy, too.

In fact, you can also share some of *your* favorite activities with your children and teach them how to participate at their own level.

Maybe they won't like all of your games any more than you do all of theirs. But you're certain to find common ground, and the older they get, the more common ground you may discover. In the process, you and your children will learn to know and enjoy one another better. When the tough times between you arise—and they will—you'll have a reservoir of good times to draw on to keep the difficulties in perspective.

10.

The Other Rules

For every game that exists, there is a list of rules and regulations that allows people to play the game successfully. When disagreements arise, the rulebook comes out and the players defer to the written word so that the game can proceed. When your children learn to play sports or games at school, in the backyard, or at the kitchen table, they are exposed to such rules. They may or may not follow them well or happily, but they will almost certainly hear them.

There is another set of rules, however, that doesn't generally appear in any book. These are the rules that have to do with being a good sport. They apply to playing fair, winning or losing gracefully, keeping your temper, abiding by the agreed-upon rules, and practicing basic courtesy. Most gym classes and physical education instructors make sportsmanship an intrinsic part of the program, but rules of courteous, fair conduct in play need a lot of reinforcement.

No one likes to lose, and most parents don't like to see their children lose. Thus the sometimes unsavory scenes that occur at youth sports league games and recreation department events, among the *adults*. Don't miss these opportunities and others like them to demonstrate what it means to keep your perspective when emotions run hot.

Your children listen with half an ear to the lists of rules and lectures on behavior, but they absorb your example. You can be sure that if you haven't yet seen your own emotional responses reenacted by your children, you will. If you have a problem being a good sport, take a breather from attending events until you figure out how to maintain your own balance and good humor in the face of any and all outcomes. You owe it not only to yourself, but to your kids, as well.

11.

Suffer With, Not From

Modern parents have developed shorthand descriptions for some of the more trying periods in a child's life, from the "terrible twos" and the "awkward preteen years" to the "rebellious teens" and "tumultuous twenties." We exchange knowing glances with other parents when our kids act their age in some predictable way. We swap our "war" stories, and talk about "surviving" their childhood. We use language of this sort to give ourselves a boost when we are frustrated, anxious, or hurting, and that's just fine.

We need to be aware, however, that such language can also have the effect of creating a strong sense of "them" and "us." In our attempts to relieve our own suffering on our kids' behalf, we can build a wall of separation. The same delineation that is meant to give us much-needed perspective creates instead an adversarial relationship. Our kids themselves become the problems we're trying to fix, instead of their struggles and challenges.

Let's admit that the last thing any child of any age needs is another adversary. Life comes equipped with more than enough of those, whether at school, on the street, or in the neighborhood. In contrast, advocates can be hard to find. When your children are hurt, confused, or just plain ornery, what they want and need more than anything else is the assurance that there is someone standing alongside, caring about what happens and giving aid and encouragement when possible.

Don't suffer *from* your kids. Suffer *with* them. Have compassion for what they're going through. Growing up is never easy, and sometimes it's dreadful. You were there once. Remember how it felt, and all that you did not understand. Your kids may not know enough to thank you now, but if you stick by them through the tough spots of growing up, you'll have the best possible foundation for a good relationship with them both now and later.

12.

Say Please and Thank You

Manners count. It is not necessary, or perhaps even desirable, for your children to memorize books of etiquette. They don't need to behave formally, nor do they need to follow some arbitrary list of scrupulous rules. Good manners are, at heart, just examples of civility—treating others with respect and courtesy—and they are learned, or not learned, most effectively at home.

Two expressions that cannot be neglected in the home epitomize good manners: "please" and "thank you." Within these words is something far more important and powerful than etiquette or politeness. "Please" and "thank you" express that the individuals matter and deserve to be treated as such. When you remind your children to say "please" and "thank you," you are preparing them to respect others.

Keep in mind that children learn most by example. You are their role model, and the individual that they will most want to emulate. Treat your children with the same degree of manners you expect from them, and their appreciation will go a long way toward influencing their behavior.

13.

Don't Just Say It, Do It

You notice that your children have slipped into the habit of spending all of Saturday morning in front of the tube. You're irked at how little they do around the house to clean up after themselves. Your children's bedrooms are a national disaster, and their eating habits are a nutritional nightmare.

The kids are clearly lazy, or so you think, and you start suggesting exercise, time outside or away from the screen, and a growing list of chores. When you're met with resistance, your suggestions become nagging, and the battle is on. There's a very good possibility that you will never find the right words to convince your children to do what it takes to shape up. In fact, words alone have very little impact on a young person. If all you intend to do is harass, you might as well save your breath.

What *does* speak to young people is what you *do*, and especially what you are willing to do with them. Do you want to pull your kids away from the television? Start putting your own imagination to work and come up with some good alternatives—sports, a martial arts class, a volunteer community activity, or a morning trip to an interesting destination. But don't simply hand over a list and command, "Choose one and get busy!" Find something that you can enjoy doing together. Locate your local state forest trails and go for a hike. Volunteer for Meals on Wheels. Wash the car together, play golf, or go to the circus. Rent a canoe or sign up for a woodworking workshop. Encourage involvement in your local sports teams, and sign up as a coach.

Do you want your children to be more responsible around the house? Work together on cleaning up the den, the garage, or the basement. Show your children how you go about making a place for everything and putting everything in its place. If you don't do it, you can hardly expect your kids to do it.

The more you build the habit of getting involved in healthy, constructive activities with your children, the more motivated and able they will be to do them. But if you're all talk, you'll unwittingly offer a powerful object lesson on inaction. Children listen best with their eyes. What you do is what they hear.

14.

Learn to Let Go

It's easy, in the interest of protecting our kids, to act as the autocrat in our own homes. We want the definitive say on what they'll wear. We want veto power over the people they spend time with. We want them to play the sports or take the private lessons that we believe will be in their best interests. We want to steer them in regard to what music they listen to, what they study, where they attend school, and what career path they pursue. We're sure that we know best—we often do—and we really don't want to see our kids fall flat on their faces, literally or metaphorically.

However, growing up and learning to take responsibility requires that children be given *some* responsibility. Step by step, children need to be given the power to make their own decisions. Obviously, you don't expect a five-year-old to choose how far from home it is okay to wander without supervision. Neither do you hand over the family car keys to a sixteen-year-old without some stringent ground rules about how, where, and whom he drives.

Empowering your children requires that you judge their maturity level and allow age- and maturity-appropriate freedom.

That doesn't mean that your children won't make poor decisions, even when you have offered ample good advice. Part of your job as a father is to make sure that the consequences of your children's mistakes, bad judgment, and disobedience are also age-appropriate and not life-threatening. People learn some of their most important lessons the hard way. If we learn them while we're young and within the circle of our parents' love and protection, we can often avoid the more disastrous, devastating consequences of irresponsibility later in life.

15.

Be Brief

Want to ensure that your child tunes you out when you deliver the important lecture? Just go on and on, beating the topic to death, repeating yourself ad nauseam, and working yourself into a self-righteous lather. You'll be certain to arouse anger, boredom, or lack of attention.

When you need to read the riot act or communicate some unpopular but necessary information or rules, be brief. Plan what you need to communicate ahead of time to prevent unnecessary elaboration. State your case clearly and concisely, without anger. Insist that your children repeat what you communicated in their own words and tell you what it means to them. Then close your mouth. You'll know soon enough if you've gotten your point across. If not, start over on a fresh occasion, and spell out the consequences of your children's potential inattention or disobedience. Good lessons bear repeating, but not by multiples in a single conversation.

16.

Create a Crash Night

Strong relationships require significant quality time. This is as true with our kids as with anyone else. It isn't enough that you live under the same roof or bring home the bacon. If you want to build a firm relationship with your children, you need to spend time with them, creating happy shared memories and a common vocabulary.

One way to make sure that you have positive time with your children is to set aside an evening a week that is just for family. Plan a no-stress time that appeals to everyone. If the whole family loves to sit and watch movies together, make that the order of the day. If you're a family that shares an outdoor sport such as golf, skiing, hiking, biking, kayaking, softball, or whatever, make a point of having a regular appointment with one another to play together. If you're chess lovers or board-game nuts, start an intra-family tournament that can go on for years.

The key to this is you and Mom. Parents may begin to feel neglected by the time that their kids reach their teens, but they often set themselves up for that disappointment. When the kids *wanted* to be with them, the parents were too busy, tired, or otherwise absorbed to make a point of weekly playtime together. It's no wonder that when the kids reach an age at which they have more choices and autonomy, they model their own behavior after the examples they've been given by their mother and father.

Every family has the potential for fun that crosses the generations. Tune in to the interests that you can happily share with your kids. Invite them to try the hobbies and activities that you find most relaxing. Ask them to teach you some of the activities that they most enjoy. In the long run, it matters less what you are doing together than that you're dedicating the time to *being* together.

If you start when your kids are young, the weekly "date" may become a tradition that thrives for years—one that may even be replicated in your children's future families. You build common ground full of funny moments and irreplaceable memories that help smooth the way for communication when times are not as fun-filled.

17.

Keep It Quiet

We all know that every couple has fights. Depending on dispositions, the character of the relationship, and the circumstances that typically lead to a fight, arguments between spouses can become loud and rancorous. It's not what anyone would choose, but it happens.

Unfortunately, in the heat of the moment, it's easy to forget that spouses with children at home have an audience when the volume goes up. While you're busy scoring points to work out your anger or using strong language to emphasize your extremely important reasoning, your children are listening. They may not understand why you're fighting or pick up the fine points of what's going on, but they won't miss the fact that Mom and Dad are not getting along. This will raise fears and cause a lot of stress.

Sometimes a good fight is needed to help clear the air. Sometimes a "discussion" simply gets out of hand. But when the arguments arise, remember your kids and give them a break. If you can't keep the volume down or the language constructive, take measures to remove yourselves from the vicinity of your kids. In some cases, talking behind closed doors is sufficient, although you can't be altogether sure. Neither can you rely on waiting until the kids are in bed. Many a child has been kept awake by parental screaming in another room, and the argument takes on the quality of nightmare.

Children should not have to suffer your adult problems. The adult choice is to find venues—and, if need be, professional help—that allow you and your life partner to spare your kids the trauma and misery of fighting parents. You may even discover that the restraint you exercise on their behalf benefits your partnership, as well.

18.

Be a Financial Advisor

It would be great if kids were born with good financial sense. In truth, some children seem to wise up early to the relative value of money, the benefits of delayed gratification in spending, and the long view for financial security. But most kids do not truly understand money without a lot of coaching and some hard lessons. As Dad, you can be one of your children's most valuable assets in the financial realm—and not because you earn a salary! They will find no more potent financial advisors than you and Mom, for better or worse. You are their earliest model for money management, both through what you espouse and what they see you do.

If you have trouble managing the financial side of life, let the fact of being a dad—and by extension, an example—be your motivation for getting your act together. Go to a professional advisor. Take a course. Check out one or more of the excellent books or videos on managing money and financial planning. In one way or another, accrue the information you need to be fiscally solid and wise, and put it into action. If your children are old enough to know that you've had your problems in this regard, make sure that they know what you're doing to remedy the situation. Insofar as you're able, begin to share what you're learning with them.

If you're an able money manager, share your good sense and philosophy with your children. Start a savings account or investment portfolio for them when they're young. Sit down with them and walk them through the basics of creating and keeping a budget. Talk to them often about the sorts of decisions you have to make in order to provide for a household and a future. It doesn't matter how little they have of their own; the smallest amounts can be used to practice good financial habits. Give them responsibility for some amount of money when they are young, and insist that they pay their own way for some of the cost of entertainment or toys. Let them put what you're teaching them to the test, and be ready to let them be disappointed at times.

Many young adults are launched into independence without a single meaningful conversation about how to handle money. Guess who often pays the price? Do your part early, and you may not have to bail them out later.

19.

Remember That They're Kids

Children do some silly things. They sometimes behave in ways that alarm or embarrass us. Some of what they do is simply annoying. Some is careless and some is dangerous. All of it has to do with being children. They have energy to burn, limited knowledge and experience, and the overwhelming need to experiment.

Keep in mind that all children develop at their own pace. Some seem to be young for their age; others seem old beyond their years. The rate at which an individual matures depends on a complex mix of nature and nurture that you may never be able to entirely sort out. What you *can* discern is how your children behave and respond in a variety of situations. With observation, you can see the areas in which your children need a lot of encouragement, and those areas in which they shine. As a parent, you can accept your children's particular maturity levels and work from there with patience and compassion.

You can and should respond as an adult to the childish behavior you see in your kids. If they disobey, you need to discipline them. If they take dangerous chances, you need to help them fully understand the dangers and do what it takes to make sure that they stop. If they behave disrespectfully or disruptively, it's your job to teach them better manners. If they're too young to behave appropriately in a given situation, it's your responsibility to make sure they do not encounter that situation until they are older. But even as you're responding in adult fashion, remember that they are, after all, only children.

Kids act like kids. It's part of what makes them so delightful and lovable, even when they infuriate you. Love them for the age that they are, even while you're guiding them into maturity. Their childhood won't last forever, and you'll miss it when it's gone.

20.

Create a Safe Place

O ne of the greatest gifts a father can offer his children is a sense of safety. Childhood fears come in many shapes and sizes. Fears of physical harm, separation, rejection, the dark, the neighbor's dog, the teacher's sarcasm—all of these can overtake children's sense of well-being. When children feel the full extent of their vulnerability—imagined or real—they face a terrifying world. No one is better equipped to allay fears than a loving, present dad.

To begin with, show your children that you will protect them from danger. If your youngsters wake in the middle of the night convinced that a stranger is in the house, in the closet, or under the bed, take the fear seriously enough to demonstrate your ability and will to keep your home safe. Look around. Tell them that all of the doors and windows are still locked. Stay with them while they fall back asleep. Explain that you have no intention of letting any harm come to them. Likewise, if your children come to you with stories of frightening events or people outside of home, respond with questions and respect. If appropriate, investigate further, and let your children know that you are doing so. If the fears are groundless, respond seriously nonetheless. Your attention and assurances, repeated as often as needed, are stepping stones to security.

You can contribute to children's security, as well, by responding consistently to them. Children's sense of safety depends on predictability. Most important to your children's sense of safety is the unshakeable knowledge of your love. Kids need to know that you'll be there, no matter what. The only way that children learn this and believe it is to experience it in one situation after another. If you make a habit of saying, "I love you, and nothing and no one can change that," you reinforce your loving actions. If you say it in the midst of conflict or discipline, your children will learn that they are loved despite any mistakes that they made or flaws that they have. Don't leave any doubt about the safety net that you provide, physically and emotionally.

21.

Share Mom with the Kids

Children inevitably change the dynamic between a husband and wife. In families with children, the romance of one plus one quickly turns into the complicated song and dance of multiples. You no longer have the luxury of being entirely wrapped up in one another, no matter how romantic or close your relationship is.

For many dads and stepdads, sharing Mom with the kids becomes a point of stress. A romantic getaway is subverted by a case of the chicken pox. An evening's heart-to-heart comes unraveled when the kid has a bad dream and needs comforting. Some individual TLC from your wife after a long workday gives way to carting the kids to events, solving problems of all sorts, and simply keeping all of the family plates spinning. With kids in the mix, you may often feel as though you've landed at the bottom of your wife's priority list.

To some extent, you have to resign yourself to the realities of child-rearing and practice new levels of patience. Kids need most of the attention that they demand while they're living at home, and moms are prone to administering it. That's part of what moms are for. But don't forget that dads have an equally vital role to play in their kids' needs. You may find that when you focus on being a primary part of the action, rather than on what you're not receiving from your wife in the midst of it, you'll enjoy your partnership in even deeper and more satisfying ways than when you were only two.

Beyond that, you can improve the situation by exercising some compassion for your wife. Chances are that when she seems to be putting you on the back burner, it's simply because you're the adult, and she rightfully believes that you can take care of yourself when she has other demands to meet. Find ways to give her a break in your attitude and you may, in the process, revive the twosome.

That isn't to say that your desire for your partner's attention must always give way. It's a privilege of an intimate relationship to expect a unique level of attention, if not always in quantity, certainly in quality. If you're feeling the pinch of your wife's distraction, tell her so. Do it in the spirit of love, understanding, and cooperation. Help her to understand, rather than simply adding to the demands on her. Talk about ways that you can *work* together to *be* together.

Child-rearing will always be demanding in the extreme. It will always require flexibility, a sense of humor, a dedicated heart, and a lot of energy. But it does not have to spell the end of closeness between you and your partner. Let it be part of what keeps you alive and laughing. Let her do what she needs to do; join in when and how you can; and make yourself the best part of her adult life.

22.

Love Them with Your Presence

In our society, we've been made to believe that happiness lies in the goods and services we consume. We are constantly told by the media that we have to have another acquisition of one kind or another. Your worth as a working man is supposedly gauged according to the income that you pull in every year. Your success as an individual is judged by what you're able to provide for your family. Your kids are exposed daily to advertising that encourages them to reinforce such messages in your thinking. "I want" or "I need" becomes a veritable litany during family time.

Well, Dad, don't you believe it. The stuff you can buy may add to the enjoyment and ease of life in some instances. At today's rate of consumption, however, it just as often makes your home overcrowded and too costly to maintain.

Think about the life you're leading. If the business of earning a "good" living and the acquiring of more goods leaves you exhausted, irritable, and away from home most of time, reconsider your choices. In terms of fathering, you can't give your children any better gift than your presence. Instead of working overtime, you might consider low-cost playtime. Instead of splashy, expensive birthday gifts, you might think about making yourself a presence at the kids' baseball games or piano recitals.

Obviously, there are all sorts of variations on ways to provide for your children, and decisions are not always yours alone. Just never forget that what your kids need and want most from you is you.

23.

Don't Blame Yourself

Because our investment in our children is enormous, their success as students, athletes, social creatures, or moral people often means as much as or more to us than our own. To varying degrees, we take their accomplishments to heart. Not only do we love them, but we are tempted to see them as extensions of ourselves.

That's why when they fail—they flunk a grade, blow a game, fall in with the wrong crowd, can't get a date—we feel responsible in some way. Your boy is arrested for shoplifting and you can't help asking, "What did I do, or fail to do, that caused him to do such a thing?" You daughter is diagnosed with anorexia, and the horror stories of psychological damage at the hands of demanding parents strike you to the core.

There's no question that the way we raise our children has a profound effect on them. The perfect parent does not exist. We all make mistakes. We all bring our own problems and neuroses to the child-rearing business, no matter how hard we may try not to. It's also true, however, that our children are individuals. They have their own wiring, experiences, thought processes, and choices to deal with. What they do with what they're born with is ultimately out of our control. Even the most dedicated psychoanalyst will concede that it's impossible to determine cause-and-effect in any definitive or exclusive way.

If your child is having problems, you'll probably never know what part you did or did not play in that outcome. To blame yourself is to lay counterproductive baggage on an already stressful situation. Unless you can pinpoint beyond a doubt some way in which you set up your child for failure—and can *do* something about it now—you and your child are both better served to start with the present and work from there.

Rather than waste your emotional energy on self-recrimination or regret, invest your time and effort in working with your child toward a turn for the better. Face the problem squarely, and help your child to do likewise. Seek professional help where appropriate. Guide your child toward a strategy for change. Most of all, be a father your child can count on for love and support without the burden of your feelings of guilt.

24.

Safeguard Mealtime

The family that eats together is becoming a thing of the past in many communities. Individual activities and schedules take priority over family dinners, and in the process, we've lost a great tradition.

Mealtime has the potential to keep everyone in touch with one another's individual concerns and interests. It can provide a peaceful anchor to a family's busy daily life. It is a place where children are encouraged to test their ideas and opinions in a safe environment. Family dinners can build a foundation of memories and shared pleasures that can sustain family relationships through the passage of time.

Because modern life is what it is, you may have to make an effort to have family mealtimes, especially after your kids start school. Begin when your children are young, and you'll have an easier time maintaining the habit as they grow. If your children are grown, set up a schedule with them so they understand that this is a priority for the family.

Don't make family dinners an opportunity to air gripes and problems. It's bad for digestion and teaches kids to dread the family table. Let positive conversation, mutual interest, and camaraderie prevail. You have the power to set the tone by your example.

Insist on table manners and gratitude to the cook or provider. Meals and table time tend to be taken for granted in modern society. Yet it takes effort to put a meal on the table. Kids need to be shown and instructed on appropriate behavior and attitudes.

Encourage your kids to get involved in figuring out how to make family mealtimes work. You're in it together, so why not act that way? Give them a piece of the action in making family "dates," choosing and preparing food, setting the table, and cleaning up. Remember to be part of the mix yourself. Don't assign the jobs and then go read the paper. This is a golden opportunity for *everyone*, not just the kids. Make the most of it.

25.

Don't Stress over the Spilled Milk

You're trying to get out the door. The kids are bickering while clearing the breakfast dishes and they've already missed the bus. Your wife is packing her briefcase, calling instructions to you from the other room. If you don't leave in the next two minutes, you'll get caught in the worst of the rush-hour traffic. And this is the moment the two older kids decide to wrestle and knock over the milk carton.

You can't help yourself. You hit the roof, push the older kids out the door without ceremony, and set the youngest wailing. When your wife rushes in, alarmed, you tell her that this would never have happened if she had planned her time better and was on the scene at the critical moment. You step angrily over the milk, follow the youngsters to the car, and load them in with a slam of the door. Your day begins, and it's very unlikely to improve, given your start.

Do you ever stop to consider why the pedestrian disasters that come with having kids feel like such a big deal? In your calmer moments, you almost certainly regret erupting like a volcano and making the whole scene worse. As an adult, it's your job to demonstrate the difference between the things that matter and those that don't. The accident doesn't spell disaster or harm for anyone. It's not the first or last time you'll be late for work.

The point is that these small catastrophes are learning experiences if you let them teach you. By your reaction, you can show your kids that people are more important than schedules, convenience, or stuff. You can point out the consequences of their actions, both from the accident itself and from the fact that no one is going anywhere until they clean up the mess they've made. And you can take a step forward yourself by choosing to respond appropriately to a minor problem with measured irritation and a rational mind. Rather than blow up over the proverbial spilled milk, rise to the occasion with fatherly perspective and wisdom.

26.

Give Driving Lessons

Your children learn from you in many ways. You may be very aware of the skills you teach them: tying shoes, riding a bike, washing the car, and, later, driving it. In these cases, you're apt to think about how and what you'll show them and what you'll expect of them. But be assured that they are learning a great deal more than what you consciously choose to teach.

Alongside the skills you teach are the attitudes that you exhibit. In the long run, your impatience and aggression behind the steering wheel, for example, will remain with their learned responses with far more persistence than the particulars of how far ahead of a turn they should begin to signal. They are watching and picking up more than you or even they realize. You are their walking, talking tutorial, not only on the how-to-dos of life, but on what to feel and how to react.

Perhaps the most powerful lessons you'll teach have to do with how you relate to your kids. These are the lessons that will influence how they raise their own kids. They will react against what they consider your mistakes and emulate what they deem your strengths.

When you react to behavior or attitudes that your children exhibit, consider where the behavior originates from. Children learn first by imitation, and you can hardly hold it against them if they give as good—or bad—as they get. If you want to raise worthy, estimable human beings, your best course of action is to take steps to be one.

27.

Demonstrate Affection

Moms have a good reputation for cuddling, kissing, and generally giving affection to their children. Historically, dads have a more confusing role, gender stereotypes notwithstanding. However, the truth is that for sons and daughters alike, dads are just as important in this department as moms.

You are the single most powerful role model in the lives of your sons. Their earliest understanding of maleness comes from you. When you freely show them physical affection, you not only say "I love you" in action; you demonstrate a fuller picture of what a man is. By loving them with hugs, kisses, and physical camaraderie, you teach them that it's okay for men to have feelings and to be honest about them. You demonstrate that emotion is not an embarrassment to men, but rather a good, normal part of being human, regardless of gender.

Your daughters will also carry the impressions of manliness set by your example into adulthood. Obviously, your displays of affection have to take into account that they are busy becoming women. You can provide a benchmark for your daughters by conscientiously demonstrating respect for their bodies. As you show them affection in ways appropriate to your role, you give them much needed affirmation, warmth, and contact with the primary male in their life. They feel more secure in themselves, and as a result, they are better equipped when they enter into relationships with possible mates.

You don't have to be someone that you are not. Some people are more demonstrative than others, and your children understand this at some level. If you tend not to be a physical person, let your gestures be small but frequent. If a bear hug comes naturally to you, be sure that your kids are the first to get one.

28.

Clean Your Room

It's amazing how, as adults, we quickly forget the mindset and challenges of our childhood. When our children make messes of their bedrooms (and sometimes spill their messes into the rest of the house), we act as though we've never known or seen anything like it. Let's be honest. Is it really so different from our own style as youths? No amount of nagging or reasoning from Mom or Dad could make you see what difference it could possibly make that you straightened up.

As the crimes and misdemeanors of childhood go, a messy room ranks pretty low on the importance scale. Granted, it's easier to keep track of homework and the pet snake with less clutter. It's also possible that a tidier space might help bring a tad more order to messy thinking. But truth be told, there are more important battles to be fought with your children than the one over a clean room.

Keep in mind that most kids have one small room to call their own—one space in which to do their own thing. You, on the other hand, may have a bedroom, study, attic, and basement. Further, if you are messy by nature, your kids will be legitimately incensed at the hypocrisy. If you want them to clean their rooms, clean your rooms, too.

Of course, you may not think that the messy room is worth the fuss. Maybe in your household, Mom is the one who is pulling her hair out over it. If so, try bringing a little sense of balance to the situation (behind closed doors). Never undermine her authority with the kids, but in private, remind her of the amazing transformation that many a young adult has gone through after moving in to his or her first apartment. Housekeeping is an acquired skill that you can model, but the lesson may not take until your kids are on their own.

29.

Talk It Out

Don't let the popular image of man retreating to his cave tempt you when conflicts arise with the kids. The silent treatment rarely accomplishes anything more than to torture the kids and give Dad more seething time. Retreat and silence are not the same as a cool-down period. If tempers flare to red-hot, by all means, take some time to regain your composure and perspective. Tell your children that's what you're doing, and give them a specific time when you'll reconvene on a more rational note. Conflict can be constructive if you turn it in that direction.

Fights with your children provide you with one of the sure signs that they're growing toward independence and adulthood. They may have a long way to go toward any semblance of maturity, but their arguments with you are often about your need to protect (and control), versus their need to pull away and be individuals. This is all part of the natural way that humans develop in families.

Of course, in the midst of what can be obnoxious, contentious behavior from your kids, it can be difficult to keep the larger picture in mind. If you aren't driven to the big outburst, you may be inclined to head for the cave. Resist it. The best way to turn conflicts into food for growth is to address them directly with your kids.

Give your children ample space to explain their points of view, and be prepared to change your mind if you've misunderstood or misjudged. Make sure that you explain yourself clearly, regardless of whether they choose to listen. And no matter what, keep the conversation firmly in the context of your love and concern for their well-being. They might not believe you now, but a lifetime of that message spoken aloud at the rough spots will make a convincing statement.

30.
Keep It Down

K ids have an uncanny ability to push our buttons. Our feelings for our children are very powerful. If they zero in on something that hurts us personally or frightens us on their behalf, we're likely to have a big reaction, often in a big voice.

You may have started raising your voice when your children were small. When one of them reached for an electrical outlet, and you said, "No," you received no perceptible response. So you barked, "*No!*" Bingo. The kid jumped in alarm and withdrew from the danger zone. It was an easy carryover when your kids reached the age at which you could reason with them. They couldn't or wouldn't understand you, you became frustrated, and instead of finding a better or different way of expressing your point, you simply repeated it at full volume. The kids didn't like an angry, yelling dad, so they toed the line.

But when children become youths and young adults, a transformation often takes place. They have their own agendas and less determination to please you at all costs. Your rules thwart their plans and desires, and they dig in their heels. Tempers flare on both sides. You raise your voice, and they—having been raised by someone who shows his emotions by yelling—follow suit.

Ask yourself honestly whether the screaming match that ensues accomplishes anything constructive. Forget the "venting" defense. You don't need to roar in your kids' faces to let off steam—and by example, teach them to do the same. You need to express yourself, and they do, too. But if you want a constructive resolution to the immediate problem, a relationship with your kids that is essentially supportive, and children who grow up with coping skills, you will do better to count to ten, breathe slowly, and lower your volume. The screaming only serves to heighten emotions and impair judgment. Control your temper and measure your response. Then you'll stand a chance of keeping the argument manageable and helpful.

31.

Make the Punishment Fit the Crime

When kids disobey or misbehave, they need discipline. As parents, when our kids do wrong, we enact punitive consequences not only as a deterrent, but also as a corrective measure. We don't just want them to stop the behavior; we want them to understand, regret, make amends, and learn to do better. For this reason, it's important that we take pains to make the punishment fit the crime.

This means that we match the discipline to the offense in terms of seriousness and content. Imagine, for example, that you tell your child not to hit the baseball in the backyard—it's too easy to accidentally break a window. The kid does it anyway, and the ball goes through the window next door. What do you do? Take away the ball and bat? Ground the child?

Consider what you're communicating when you make your decision. Taking away the sports equipment may protect the windows in the future, but it doesn't teach your child the real-life cost of such carelessness. Grounding your child will almost certainly offend the kid's sense of justice—it has nothing to do with what happened, and serves to make staying at home a punishment.

The more meaningful response to this particular disobedience would be to insist that the child pay for the damage out of allowance or savings, and make a personal apology to the neighbor. The former hits where it hurts for most kids—just think how much bubble gum could be purchased for the price of a broken window! The latter puts a face on the thoughtlessness of the child's action. A real person was on the other side of that pane of glass. That person could have been injured. There's something very powerful about having to own up, eyeball to eyeball, and see firsthand how you've affected another human being.

Some disobedience is less damaging. Some is much more serious. The point is that if you overreact, you offend your child's sense of fairness and build more resentment than repentance. If you choose a punishment that doesn't relate to the trouble at hand, you lose the opportunity for a valuable lesson that your child can understand. If you shrug off the behavior as unimportant or not worth the effort to respond to, you teach your child that disobedience isn't a big deal—a lesson you will certainly regret later.

You can be sure you'll have to deal with disobedience and misbehavior as your children grow. By far, the least stressful and most effective way to deal with it is to answer it consistently with discipline that teaches the lesson you want your child to learn.

32.

Let the Punishment End

When it's time to discipline, live up to your promises. Best case, you've made clear to your children what constitutes disobedience and what the results of misbehavior are. If the kids put you to the test and break the rules, you owe it to their character and their future to follow through. There's no better way to build a solid sensibility in them about right and wrong, and there's no stronger means for them to develop consequential thinking.

If you're angry or frustrated enough, however, it can be difficult to let the matter drop. Be careful, Dad. When you hang on to your anger beyond the initial response, you teach your children a very different lesson from the one related to their disobedience. You teach them that your love and friendship are conditional. No child thrives—and no parent-child relationship grows—under the threat of rejection.

Do the hard work of making crime and punishment completely clear to your kids as soon as they're old enough to understand. Keep revising the particulars as they grow and their lives change, so that everyone knows where they stand on the subjects of obedience and safety. Let there be one constant: that you love them and want the best for them, no matter what and no matter how angry you may feel. When they know that they stand on that firm ground, they can keep the business of discipline in perspective and grow to respect it.

33.

Be Careful
What You Say to Others

In the midst of child-rearing, our kids figure large in our thinking and, often, in our conversation with friends and extended family. We tell "cute" stories about what the kids say or do, express our pride in their shining moments, share our concerns about them, and seek the wisdom and advice of others on how to deal with their troubles. However, sharing has its pitfalls, and our kids can wind up as victims.

Choose the time and place for confiding with care. Many children have been humiliated by what they overheard being related about them. Your anecdotes may feel like an invasion of their privacy. If your children tell you that your praise, teasing, or revelations in public embarrass them, take it seriously and respect them enough to give them a say in what you say.

Choose your audience with care, as well. Too often, people make the concerns and stories about others and their kids grist for the rumor mill. A story about your daughter's bad behavior might turn into a juicy piece of gossip that paints her in a bad light and comes back to haunt her in the form of biases or labels. Furthermore, your confidant may be someone who has a problem with discretion altogether. You may hear yourself quoted by them to your children. Generally speaking, this is not a good way for your kids to hear what you're thinking or saying about them.

You have privileged information about your children. The way that you treat that honor communicates a great deal to them about your respect and love for them. A small confidence in the wrong setting or to the wrong person can lead to a big hurt. Think before you talk about your kids. They need to know that they can trust you.

34.

Make Room for Fido

What child doesn't want a pet? No matter how removed we are from a state of nature in our daily lives, we continue to reach out to animals for some sort of relationship. Rare is the child who doesn't conceive a great longing for some sort of critter. There is a fundamental difference between bonding with humans and bonding with pets, but there is an equally fundamental difference between bonding with pets and bonding with dolls, for example. Toys are just toys, without intrinsic quirks and behaviors, and without the capacity for pleasurable responses or such traits as loyalty. Children and pets experience a living, everyday relationship that can be as strong as the children's relationships to kin or friends.

After months of imploring you for a pet, you may finally capitulate. A dog or cat arrives in the household. After a brief period of euphoria, the work begins. If your children were serious about wanting the pet, you can insist that they be serious about taking responsibility for that pet and looking after it. Pets provide a wonderful, ongoing opportunity to teach children dependability and perseverance. Pets need housebreaking, some level of obedience training, feeding, brushing, exercise, and attention. They need safekeeping from escape into traffic and rescue from trees and other animals. Children can be taught to take an active part in all of this.

As pets mature, they gain a solid and predictable place in the family. They provide solace when children are lonely or blue. They provide comedy when times are dull or heavy. They allow children a sense of ownership and companionship. When you not only allow the animal in, but also let your children take it on, you soften the edges of life and give your family a treat.

35.

Expect the Unexpected

Kids are full of surprises, and on a good day, we all agree that this is part of what makes them so charming and delightful. But when you've got tickets to Disney World and your kid wakes up on travel day with a raging flu, you're likely to find the surprise less than a delight. You can be sure that such things will happen. If you've been a dad for long, you've already negotiated your share.

One of the best ways to take the sting out of the unpredictability of life with children is to assume things will not go as planned. The kids will get sick or injured, no matter how well you've trained them to wash their hands and stay away from dangerous situations. They will get into fights with the kids down the street, even though you and Mom are ardent pacifists. They will vomit in your lap, turn up after curfew, flush the teddy bear down the toilet, and feed the fish from the living room tank to the neighbor's cat. These are the things that kids do. No one has ever raised a family without such surprises. No one ever will.

You can also cultivate your sense of humor. Of course, you may need to take a long view and more than a few aspirin to do it. But in truth, most of the surprises that your children hand you will eventually become funny stories for you to relate to new parents who are stressed over the usual stuff of parenting.

Before you let the surprises overtake your temper or your nervous system, try shaking your head, giving one good sigh, and then sneaking in a chuckle. Life's too short to always know what's next. Enjoy the fact that kids prevent such an occurrence.

36.

Don't Look for Clones

As gratifying as it may be to hear that your child is "a chip off the old block" when your child is looking good and behaving well, it can feed into a way of thinking that has a definite downside. While your kids may have their share of traits that resemble yours, your children are not you, and they never will be. You and their mother have contributed to their hardwiring in distinct ways, but your kids have a different nuclear family from your nuclear family; they live in a different era, have different emphases in education, enjoy a new generation of entertainment, and are exposed to a different environment. Deep in your fatherly soul, you may have a desire for your kids to look, think, play, live, work, and choose as you do. If so, get over it. Unless you can, you're in for frustration and disappointment.

Recognize that each child you raise is utterly him- or herself, and this is what makes every child so special. Certainly, you have an enormous influence on your children. By loving them for who they are and encouraging each according to talents, interests, foibles, and strengths, you have the inestimable privilege of launching a brand *new* person into the world.

Resist the clone syndrome. Being a good dad does not mean treating your children as lumps of clay just waiting to be fashioned in your own image. Such an attitude eventually alienates them, and leaves you wondering why you don't have a better relationship with your grown kids. Get excited instead about how different from you they are and how much you will gain from knowing them, now and later.

37.

Remember Who's Who

What is it that sends some fathers off the deep end in the middle of a junior sports event? One minute, everyone is having a friendly community afternoon. The next, Dad is ready to punch the ref, throttle the kids, and sever all relations with his neighbor (whose kid just scored a questionable point for the opposing team). In some cases, it's simply an irrepressible competitive streak, which needs to be controlled. Sometimes, though, it's more than that. It's a matter of living vicariously—trying to live out your own dreams through the talents and pursuits of your children. It can manifest itself in academics, the arts, dating, or employment.

Your feelings for your children run soul-deep. You see yourself in them, and you want the best for their lives. You're tempted to identify with their successes and failures. All of this is natural and normal. When you allow such feelings to become about fulfilling ambitions for your child, however, you're treading on dangerous ground.

Children benefit from their parents' encouragement as they experiment with different skills. Part of being young is the need to experiment—to pick up and put down a variety of activities and ambitions in the spirit of self-discovery and exploration. When you provide the opportunities for your children to do this, you are giving them information to make intelligent choices that reflect who they really are as they enter adulthood. Alternatively, when you zero in on the pursuits that suit your own dreams and push your children to choose accordingly, you are stealing some of that precious freedom that ought to be the best part of youth.

Kids need to know that you can be proud of them, whether or not they choose what you might choose. They need to know that you stand beside them proudly because they are true to themselves, not because they've modeled themselves after your dreams. Let your dreams be your own, and revel in the mystery of who your children will become.

38.

Let the Phone Ring

F amily time can be hard to come by and even more difficult to sustain. The same technology that has created instant communication, high-speed travel, and an appliance for every chore has invaded our most private lives. You can choose to spend the day, evening, or weekend at home with the family and find yourself as busy with e-mail, telephone calls, and people with something to sell as you would be at your place of business.

Concentrated, undistracted time with your children—quality time—is essential if you want to know and enjoy your kids fully. Stress-free time is optimal, but even at home, it's at a premium for most people today. To create it and ensure it, you need to make some choices. For the sake of your relationship with your kids, and for a life that has balance and perspective, try letting the answering machine do its job for a day. Neglect the e-mail for twenty-four hours. Leave the television and the computer off.

Once you've cleared the air of distractions and stress-producers, you can get your quality time. Play games as a family. Read a book together. Build a tree house together. Enlist the whole family in the cooking of a meal. Eat together at the table, on the lawn, or even in the tree house, knowing that nothing is going to interrupt you. Spend a weekend working on an all-family project. Go on a mini-vacation for no other reason than to be together having fun.

Creating such concentrated times not only builds your relationship with your kids, it tells them that they're important enough to you that you'll lay aside your other concerns to be with them. Give yourself that luxury. You won't regret it.

39.

Leave Them at Home

How often have you seen parents doing battle with children in a store, at a museum, in a nice restaurant, or at an adult dinner party? "Stop running!" "Keep your voice down!" "Don't touch that!" The kid becomes distraught or angry, the parents are stressed and embarrassed, and the people around them are frankly less than pleased to be in their company.

More often than not, the children are not the problem. They are just acting like children. The parents may not be the problem, either. They're doing the best they can to keep the kids in hand and minimize the disruption to the other adults in the vicinity. The problem originates with the decision to bring the children into situations intended for adults. The duration of the outing may be too long for the children's attention span, there may not be anything interesting for the children to do, or the hour may be so late that the kid is just flat-out exhausted.

Be fair to your kids. Don't expect or demand that they rise to adult occasions except in the rarest of circumstances. If you're gathering with other parents and everybody is including their children, fine. Otherwise, if you can't get a baby-sitter or entice a relative to do the job, stay at home or find venues that are appropriate. Go to restaurants designed for families with kids of all ages. Make your shopping trips short and to the point. Choose times when the kids have the energy to deal with what you're doing. Be the adult in the situation who knows the limits and has the good sense to honor them.

40.

Let Kids Be Kids

As a father, your mission is to guide your children into responsible, self-actuating adulthood. They don't come by good judgment, integrity, motivation, or character without help and discipline. The chores you assign, the rules you establish, the consequences you enforce, and the examples you set are serious, necessary business. They are a critical part of the way you love your kids. So, too, are the opportunities that you give them to be involved in extracurricular activities and the structure you provide for them to study and learn.

Yet, we can often get caught up in the desire to fill all of our children's hours with too much structured time. The fact is that the one commodity children today are missing and desperately need is unstructured playtime. Children today suffer an unprecedented level of stress-related ailments and physical problems, and it just may be that we're setting them up for it. In the interest of keeping our kids busy, involved, and out of trouble, we may be structuring them right out of self-discovery, imagination, healthy activity, and freedom.

Given a wholesome environment and appropriate supervision—which is to say that you know where they are, whom they're with, and essentially what they're up to—children have a remarkable ability to entertain themselves. They take naturally to role-playing, exploring, inventing challenges, and creating games. With very little involvement and guidance from you, they become entranced with the natural world and the life lessons to be learned from it. They learn to get along with one another, find things that they do well, and discover what captures their interest.

As you consider how best to give your children a good shot at a meaningful, satisfying adult life, remember the value and wonder of childhood. They may only have the chance for such unfettered, magical play through the few short years of dependence on you. Give yourself, your wallet, and especially your children a break. While they're kids, let them be kids.

41.

Give Them the Credit

The awards ceremony is over. Your hand's been pumped by several parents and a number of teachers. Even the principal has singled you out to tell you what a spectacular kid you have, and what a pleasure it is to have that child in the school.

You are full of pride and self-satisfaction. It's a great bonus to parenting when your kids thrive at whatever they're doing. But who are you accepting the praise for? Is it for your child, or yourself?

Just as you can't blame yourself for your children's failures and slip-ups, you can't credit yourself when they do well. Your children have figured out what to do with what they have been given. Parenting is about maintenance and delivery. You're not the source or the reason for your children's successes. You're responsible for being the best father that you can be, and for giving your children the best that you have to offer. The outcome belongs to your kids.

When you're tempted to blush and be modest at praise for your children, reconsider. If it were someone unrelated to you, how would you respond? Probably with a big smile and agreement. "You're right, the kid really did a good job!" you might say. So say it already. Give credit where credit is due—most of all to your child.

42.

Laugh with Them, Not at Them

Kids can be almost unbearably cute sometimes. Their naiveté and quirky ways of interpreting the world can tickle your funny bone and warm your heart. They come out with some amazing truths and equally stunning mistakes. They do uninhibited things that simultaneously crack you up and make you wistful for childhood. And they provide you with some hilarious stories to tell over an adult dinner. When you love the childish things in children, life is never dull or too serious.

Unfortunately, it's easy to take endearing actions or statements from your children and turn them into jokes at their expense. Children often fail to see the humor in what they say or do. They're just being their own young selves. It takes an adult perspective to see the joke. A fine line exists between delighting in your children's innocent gaffes and foibles, and making fun of them. It's worth every ounce of your self-restraint to avoid overstepping that line.

Children need to know that you respect them and take them seriously. Much frustration and hurt are visited on children by parents who miss the serious intent of the kids' funny outbursts. If you make them the butt of your laughter often and long enough, many children will either turn inward or become clownish in their behavior. In either event, it's self-defense.

By all means, embrace the delightful moments in your children and enjoy a chuckle when they aren't aware. But also be sure to communicate that you take them seriously as you find them—young, relatively ignorant, and untried—and respect them for the youthful, growing individuals that they are.

43.

Support the Authority of Others

It's part of your role as Dad to protect and defend your children when they are wronged. When they know that they can depend on your support and protection, they feel safe and confident. They need and want that from you.

It's possible, too, that you will want to step in to protect even when *your* children are wrong or accused of wrongdoings. You want to protect your children from long-term marks against their names. You want to save them from the tougher hard knocks. And you want to see false accusers put in their place. Often, the accusers are people in authority—school administrators, police officers, other children's parents, coaches, or shopkeepers. In your protective mode, you may be tempted to lash out at those authorities.

It is in such times of stress that you need a sense of perspective and proportion. It's natural for most parents to believe that their own children are innocent. When accusations fly, no matter what the source, most parents are inclined to assume the best at first.

There's nothing wrong with that. It shows an intrinsic respect for and belief in your children. In fact, they may be innocent, and your support gives them the confidence to defend themselves. However, sometimes your children are in the wrong, or their innocence is marginal because they're in the "wrong place at the wrong time"— and with the wrong kids. The misdemeanors of their chosen pals have landed on their heads.

In either case, there's more at stake than your children's defense at the moment. There is their ability to see themselves in ethically and morally realistic terms. You give your children a good shot at growing into mature, honest individuals when you teach them to respect people in authority whose responsibility it is to bring wrongdoing to light and put a stop to it.

This doesn't mean that you bow to injustice or let a dishonest or mistaken accuser rule the day. It does mean that you support what the authority stands for, even when you need to go to bat for an innocent kid or deal with an unworthy authority figure. It also means that when your children are in the wrong, you hold them responsible and let the consequences run their course. Some of the most important lessons in life can be learned the hard way as a child. Be thankful when it's relatively minor with short-term consequences. It may just save your child more serious trouble in adulthood.

44.

Plan Family Vacations Together

Have you ever gone to the trouble and expense of planning a great vacation for the family, only to have your children spend the entire getaway complaining or bickering? You feel as if you've wasted your time and money, and they agree. What should have been fun and relaxing turns into one more stress-producer.

Don't do that more than once. For the next family gig, get your children involved. Make it part of the event to research, choose, and plan a vacation together. Give the gang a budget and a time frame. Explain to them the limits and challenges that you have to take into account in order to make the trip viable for everyone. When they come up with ideas that are unrealistic, make sure that they have the opportunity to discover why, whether it has to do with money, time, or individual challenges. It's amazing how realistic children can become when they know the facts instead of simply being told, "It's not possible," or "It's too expensive," or "It wouldn't work."

You may want to start small and move on to more extensive getaways after you've had the experience of a group plan. Or you may want to limit the kids' involvement to an array of choices prescreened by you and Mom. Or you may simply choose to negotiate the details of a pre-selected spot so that everybody feels as if there's something in it for them. In any case, you'll give your children a vested interest in the success of the vacation. After all, they're partly responsible for where you go and what you do when you get there. In the case of disagreements at the planning stage, be democratic and vote. Assure the losing voters that they'll get their turn if everyone pitches in for a good time.

Such a system may sound like a lot of trouble. In practice, however, it doubles the pleasure of family plans. The kids feel important and trusted, and you all develop a new understanding of who each person is and what they value and enjoy. Best of all, you build memories and relationships that you can cherish.

45.

Plant a Garden

Downtime with your kids sometimes takes on a tedious, frayed-nerve edge that leaves you longing to go back to the office. This is especially true when your children are at an age that you find difficult to relate to. Feeling guilty for not particularly enjoying the company of these children whom you love so deeply can feed a short temper and exacerbate your edginess. Let's face it: Kids are not always the delights that we expect them to be.

Make your time with your kids more interesting by involving them in something you enjoy. Younger children love the presence and attention of their parents. If you start an activity with the intention of including them, you're almost certain to get a positive response. Plant a garden or build a fishpond. Make a play area or even wash the car. Teach them the rudiments of a game that you love, whether it's golf, basketball, chess, or bridge. If you have age-appropriate jobs or lessons for them, let them stop when their attention span runs out, and you'll have a success on your hands.

In the case of older children and teenagers, your best bet is to concentrate on an activity that already means something to them. Does your son have an avid interest in cars? Go in search of the "perfect" car, even if it's a few years too soon. Daydream together and talk real sense about what's involved in buying and operating your own vehicle. If your teenage daughter wants to redo her room, make it a joint effort, start to finish. Plan it, buy for it, and execute it as a team, or with help from siblings and appropriate "experts."

The marvel in structuring your time with your kids in such a way is that you get to know them as you never could otherwise, and they get to know you. You create legitimate camaraderie and common interests that could very well last a lifetime.

46.

Be Predictable

Spontaneity is a wonderful thing in a dad. What a blast to have an ordinary weekend turned on its head when Dad packs everyone up on the spur of the moment to spend the day at the beach. Or to wake up (on a school day!) to the smell of Dad's famous waffles. But some surprises are not a treat, nor do they serve a child's sense of security. In fact, they add stress and instability to your family's life.

For example, you make life tough on your kids and yourself when you say one thing and do another. If your words don't reflect your actions—if you espouse one set of values and regularly live by another—your children not only come to doubt your words, but learn by example to be hypocrites. So, too, they learn by example when you make promises and fail to follow through with any frequency. The disappointment and discouragement that your children experience can translate into a growing lack of respect, both for you and for responsibility in general. This can take its toll on the quality of your home life and your relationship with them.

Children want and need boundaries. It's up to you and your wife to make the rules and enforce them, for the sake of your children's safety and character. When you set up parameters for your children, they need for you to uphold those limits consistently. If you take the lazy way out and let disobedience go, or if you change the rules at will to serve your convenience or whim, you subvert the business of discipline and leave your kids unsettled, frustrated, and confused.

Kids thrive in a consistent, predictable environment, even when it means that they have to take their lumps for misbehaving. Your predictability gives them a firm place to stand. It gives them a yardstick against which they can measure their choices. And it offers them a safe place of retreat from a world that hands out more than a few unpleasant surprises in life.

Be your children's Rock of Gibraltar. Give them the gift of stability by showing consistent, dependable values, words, and behavior. It may seem like a lot of work at times, but in truth, such predictability makes home life—and all of life—far less stressful.

47.

Explain Why

Some parents may start pulling their hair out at about the time their kids learn to ask, "Why?" It starts for a lot of children at about age two, and it continues into young adulthood. Sometimes you're dealing with honest ignorance and curiosity. Kids really don't know why you've told them what you've told them: why you've said no when they wanted something; why you've said "do this" when they had "that" in mind. At other times, you're faced with their unwillingness to accept what you say. They want what they want, and you're telling them that they can't have it or do it, so they test your determination by asking, "Why?"

As parents, we can grow weary of answering why. It tends to be repeated a lot at certain stages of a child's development. But you shouldn't let your frustration with its repetition stop you from answering. The first time your children ask why on a particular subject, assume that it's an honest question. The "because" you offer is an important part of your children's education. The kids need to know, first of all, that there *is* a "because," and if you can't provide one, you might need to ask *yourself* why. Your children also need the information that you provide, even if they don't have the prior knowledge or experience to entirely understand it. Such knowledge is often built on a series of questions to their parents.

When the questioning continues—you've answered at least once, and the kids won't let it go—you might need to try different ways of explaining yourself. Believe it or not, what makes sense to your adult ears may not translate into children's ways of understanding the world. You must find an explanation that your kids can relate to. Try again, and see if you can draw an analogy to something within their experience that makes your answer more intelligible.

The time will come, of course, when you know perfectly well that your kids understand what you're saying. They just don't want to hear it, and hope to wear you down. At that point, you're well within the limits of fairness to say: "I've explained this several times now. I'll explain it one more time. If you have questions about what I say, ask them now and I'll answer. But then the discussion is over. I mean what I say, and it's not going to change. So don't bother to ask again unless you have something new to add."

Then stick to your guns. Your children may not like it, but over time, if you're consistent in similar situations, they will learn when to quit. You'll receive more legitimate questions than questions that test you. The former are always worth answering.

48.

Remember School Days

Remember your school days, when bullies looked like gangsters, teachers seemed older than God, and yesterday's friends were the next day's tormentors? Okay, maybe your school experiences were better than that and your memories are rosy. But if you didn't have your share of hard knocks and tough times, you're one in a million. Of course, by the time your kids hit school age, your memories may be dim. That's where some empathetic recall can come in handy.

For children, small school problems often feel bigger than life. Their relative powerlessness can make their fears overwhelming. When your kids take the brave step of confiding in you about aspects of school that are trying to them, take off your "dad shoes" long enough to remember—*really* remember—what it was like to be six or ten or fifteen. Remember the agony of being shy and having to stand up in front of the class; or the terror of being called on when you hadn't done your schoolwork; or the feeling of betrayal when your buddy turned against you or left you out. At the time, you didn't know and wouldn't have believed that your unhappiness would pass. You only knew that you hurt. Feel the pain again, even if only for a moment. That's what your kids are going through, and they need a sympathetic ear. Only when you can sympathize are you ready to be wise, all-knowing Dad.

Sometimes it's enough that you let your kids vent without judging them or belittling their feelings at all. Simply saying, "I know it hurts. I'm so sorry that you're going through this," is all that they really want or need. Sometimes, though, your ability to remember and share your own childhood with them can offer much-needed hope. For example, talk about the kid who stole your math homework and the trouble it landed you in. This lets them know that it happens to everyone as a kid, even Dad. Perhaps that kid went on to be thrown out of school, while you took first honors in math. Tell this to your kids also, and they will have a sense of eventual justice.

Obviously, not all school-day troubles have such happy endings. But if you've lived to tell the tale, you can at least assure your kids that you, too, once had such worries. They lasted for a while, they ended, and they ceased to be important. They were all part of growing up, for you and every other adult your kids know. In the meantime, you've told them that their feelings matter and are understandable. You may or may not have good advice to offer. They may or may not want to hear it. But you've been a good listener and a sympathetic friend, and that's worth its weight in gold.

49.

Go One on One

There's no substitute for individual attention. When you look your child in the eye and demonstrate that no one and nothing else is on your mind, you say loudly and clearly that your kid is uniquely important to you. It's the rare child who doesn't rise to such an occasion with pleasure and appreciation, even though you may never hear it spoken. But such attention takes effort. You can't fake it. Kids can spot a fake a mile off.

When your child comes to you for advice, to tell a story, or even to chatter, make a point of laying aside what you're doing to fully pay attention. The conversation may take only sixty seconds, but in that single minute, you may learn more about what your child thinks and feels than you would in countless interactions in which you give only half an ear and little eye contact.

If your child needs to talk for a stretch at a time when you can't be interrupted to such an extent, tell the child, "I'm very interested in what you're saying. Give me a minute (or half an hour or until three o'clock), and then we can sit down together." You may miss the moment—the child may lose interest before the appointed time arrives—but at least you've registered your genuine interest.

If you work at home, you may have to spell out the times when you are available and the times when you are not. A home office presents particular challenges to family relations, but the challenge is negotiable, provided you're able to close the door on work when family time arrives. As long as your kids know that you will be fully theirs at some point, the restrictions do no harm to a close, vital connection to them. And an occasional invitation into the office, one at a time, can actually give you opportunities that aren't otherwise available.

For most parents, one-on-one time can be remarkably difficult to engineer at home. There's no reason why you can't make regular—even weekly—dates with each of your kids for time alone. A walk or a run, a ride in the car, a meal at a local spot, or a trip to the post office can offer precious moments alone. Whatever it takes, make a point of giving each child the gift of yourself, without Mom or siblings along. This may eventually be the venue for some of the most significant conversations you'll have.

50.

Spell Out the Consequences

The concept of responsibility is not an easy one. In fact, some people never get it, no matter how long they live. Kids stand a better chance of understanding that they're responsible for their own choices and actions if the lessons start early and continue consistently. The most effective place for them to get the message is at home.

This means that you should give your children responsibility—the freedom to make choices. On a basic level, they should be responsible for listening to what they've been told: "Stay away from the stove," or "Keep your seat belt buckled."

The trick to teaching more than simply, "Do as I say," is explaining the consequences. "If you touch the stove, you'll burn your fingers." It only takes one time for a child to learn what it means when something is hot enough to burn. After that, most children take some responsibility for avoiding burning surfaces. When you subsequently warn them about something that will hurt them, they're more likely to believe you and take responsibility there, as well. These represent the earliest, most elementary lessons in responsibility, but they begin an important process—as long as you spell out the consequences and follow through.

An older child can be given responsibility for coming home on time, for carrying the permission slip to school and handing it in to the right person, for setting up the schedule for karate lessons, or for taking care of a pet. All responsibilities carry ramifications for neglecting them—some imposed by you (for coming home late, for instance), and others built into the task itself (if the permission slip doesn't arrive on time, they miss an opportunity). Sometimes kids neglect their responsibilities and are saddled with consequences that you could fix. Unless it's a matter of saving the poor dog from starvation and thirst, don't do it. They need to feel the discomfort that goes along with not fulfilling their responsibilities.

Teaching responsibility is a straightforward part of being a dad. If you stick to it when matters are relatively minor, you may save yourself big headaches when the consequences of your kids' choices are much more serious.

51.

Love Your Children's Mother

Your children's mother holds a precious place in their hearts and minds. A positive, healthy relationship with her is an important part of their emotional well-being. If you have a happy marriage with her, it's probably easy to love and support her in her mothering. When the kids are mad at her, you find ways to uphold her and honor her. When she's at her wits' end with the kids, you move to the forward line and give her a break while she marshals her resources for the next go-round. Because of the strong bond you maintain as partners, you simplify the business of parenting by being a united voice and a loving support to one another. You give your children the gift of a secure, relatively uncomplicated home environment.

However, even the happiest marriage hits rocky territory at times. When the friction between you and your partner gets heavy enough, it's tempting to look to the kids for support. You want to vent your negative feelings, and you want them on your side. Additionally, you want some positive emotional responses for yourself, and the kids are often ready to give them, especially when they sense the tension between you and their mom. It makes them at least as uncomfortable as it does you. Putting your children in the middle, complaining to them, or asking them to choose sides in an adult problem is not only unfair to them and to their mother, it's destructive to the family structure. You cannot effectively parent when you're busy trying to make your children your allies. And children cannot avoid fears of separation and loss when they're dragged into their parents' conflicts.

You owe it to your children to give your best effort to loving and respecting their mother. You may be enraged with her. You may even be divorced from her. But she still holds the position of Mom. Your kids need some kind of relationship with her (except in extreme circumstances) that allows them to include her in their lives and love her themselves. Don't try to get even. In such a case, your first concern should be your children. Most times, they're wiser than you know. If you behave with dignity and show respect for their mom, despite all, they'll see you for who and what you are.

52.

Extend Yourselves as a Family

Most of the stuff that gets us riled up in family life has to do with a very small circle of concerns, many of them not extending beyond our own front door. Because family life tends to be so intimate and interconnected, it's hard to bring a larger perspective to bear. Our feelings become concentrated and intense, and we judge our troubles relative only to ourselves.

One of the most effective means of getting yourself and your family out of a narrow frame of mind is to put yourselves, as a family, in situations where you are serving others. Opportunities abound for volunteering your efforts to do good for someone other than yourselves.

Most communities, for example, offer ways to be involved in improvement projects, whether they focus on cleanup days, recycling drives, municipal projects, or facility refurbishing. If kids are old enough to pick up trash, wield a paintbrush, tie up newspapers, or weed a garden plot, they can dig in, especially with you at their side.

Charity efforts also welcome your volunteer support. Soup kitchens, clothing and food banks, homeless shelters, and collection centers often depend on volunteers to do the nitty-gritty work. Some towns develop community service opportunities especially geared for young people. And of course, there are the well-known national organizations with local chapters—the American Red Cross, Meals on Wheels, the Salvation Army, and others—which routinely include volunteers in their efforts.

The great plus for a family that gets involved as a group—aside from the joy of doing something meaningful together—is the sense of perspective gained. It's hard to get too bent out of shape over who finished the ice cream when you've spent an evening ladling soup and dishing salad for the genuinely down-and-out. When you start slipping into pettiness, you have shared experiences to which you can refer that help you to regain your footing. Don't let your family's world stop at the front door. Reach out. You'll be happier for it.

53.

Share the Load Fairly

Most families, if they include more than one child, have a mix of temperaments and ages that can cause friction when it comes to individual responsibilities at home. This is an area where some family planning can go a long way toward smoothing tension. In fact, frustrations are often warranted. Some kids really don't pull their share of the load, and the other kids rightfully want and demand a fair shake. If they don't have your help and intervention, it's not surprising that they lose their cool.

If you make chores a part of your family's day-to-day activities, go the extra distance to make it evenhanded, and devise a system of accountability. You may want to get as organized as making a chart with duties, time frames, and names on it—and make sure Mom and Dad are included.

Don't let chores and individual responsibility make your family life unpleasant. Manage it well, and everyone will gain.

54.

Be a Good Sounding Board

One of the challenges of parenting is facing the moment when your children cease to tell you all that's on their minds. Most young children, given a chance and a listening ear, will spill all. But one of the ways that children mature is to keep some of their thoughts and feelings to themselves; to have secrets and choose people other than their parents as confidants. It's an important step in the process of separating.

A good parent, however, wants to keep the door open to communication. Granted that your children no longer tell you everything, or even much; you still want to have a relationship with enough trust and openness that they will sometimes choose to make you the listener. You may be on the receiving end of ideas, frustrations, early stirrings of love, or fears. Regardless of the content, your children's decision to talk to you is a privilege and a trust.

Honor the gift of your children's trust. It can be difficult to listen well. You may have wisdom you want to impart, or sense dangers that you want to protect them from. You may be privy to information that makes your toes curl. You're tempted to say, "That was bad," or "Don't be an idiot," or "I don't know what you see in that person." What you communicate is that you've judged your children and found something wanting about them, their friends, or their interests. Kids react with less than enthusiasm when they feel judged, just as you do. So don't be surprised if you find the door of interaction slammed in your face.

Be a good sounding board. Listen without judgment. Let your kids test ideas out loud with you. Let them explore their feelings. Allow them the space to be young and presumptuous. Show them the respect that you want to be shown, and they'll continue to seek you out when they're in need of a listening ear.

55.

Take Pictures

Memories are important. They add texture and vitality to the present. They allow the past to live on in some way. They also provide an excellent frame of reference when we are raising our children. We sometimes feel frustrated at the lack of progress we seem to make in shaping the character and behavior of our kids. But the truth is that we're often further along than we realize. We just have short memories of where we started.

Get into the habit of keeping records of the various phases of your children's and your family's life. Take pictures and put them in good enough order so that you can enjoy looking back at them from time to time. Include short captions on the back of snapshots that give time and place and some comment about the situation. It often takes very little to remember an entire scene and what was going on, when you provide yourself with some small prompt.

If you're someone who likes to set down your thoughts on paper, keep a simple journal in which you record some of the important issues and events in the lives of your kids. Looking back on what you've written and remembering how much has changed over the years may help you put your feelings, and your kids' choices as young adults, in perspective.

Cherish your memories enough to keep mementos and records that will help you preserve them. They are a gift.

56.

Do as I Do, Not as I Say

This is not a news flash. Kids learn far more effectively from what you do than from what you say. If you're pulling out your hair over how often you have to give your children "time out" because they will not listen to you, you may be due for a time out of your own.

Try an experiment. Every time you find your frustration level rising with your kids' misdeeds, take the time to pinpoint specifically what the problem behavior is. If it's rudeness, take note. When you speak to your children in the midst of frustration, do you make courtesy a habit? Possibly not. Your fuse is spent, and you let them have it in no uncertain terms.

Here's the rub: Often, your children will lose their manners most noticeably when they, too, are frustrated. Someone has bossed them around, or won't listen to them, or has taken something that belongs to them. You've shown them how to handle that particular emotion: Lose your cool and act out. Unless you take the time to talk to them and give them an opportunity to explain *why* they're behaving as they are, you won't know that. But if you listen to them in such a context, you not only gain understanding and a clue about how to direct them, you show them, by your example, how you can be frustrated and civil at the same time.

Instead of letting your children's bad behavior become a big, bad deal in your household, get to the bottom of it with them and do some soul-searching in yourself. We teach our children, but they teach us, too. Be the student of good behavior and character you want your children to be, and they'll follow in your footsteps without even knowing it.

57.

Be the Buffer with Grandparents

In the midst of raising kids, many parents find themselves in the sandwich situation. While their children are still at home and demanding the predictable amount of attention, their parents are aging and in need of an increasing amount of energy, as well. In some cases, the oldest generation moves in with kids and grandkids when their capacity for independent living dwindles. In others, although they have a separate living situation, they look to their children for more and more support and help.

Caught in the middle, with compelling demands on both sides of the equation, you may begin to feel like the rope in a tug of war. Unfortunately, your children sometimes take the fallout. You understand that your parents' time is limited. You want to do your best for them. But your time and energy also have their limits, and meeting all of your parents' demands may mean giving your kids less than your best. In addition, senility, the frustrations of losses, and fears can make interactions with the older folks problematic for you and your children. Grandparents can cease to be the benign, generous, once-removed presence in your kids' lives, and instead be an intrusion.

You can lessen the stress, first of all, by taking the time to think through and know your priorities. Is your parent terminally ill? Are your children at an age when they need a lot of you? Are you dealing with a recently widowed mother or father? Does one of your children have special needs or a particular issue at present? All of these factors can affect how you prioritize your family involvement. So, too, should the fact that your children depend on you alone for parenting, while your parents may have other children than you who can and should share the burden. There may also be alternative care possibilities for some of the daily demands that come with your parents' advanced age.

You will also reduce the stress of the situation if you communicate clearly with your children about what's going on with their grandparents, why it's important to be involved with them, and the underlying causes of problematic interactions. Your children can become an active part of the process. This keeps your own family working together, even while teaching the kids something about loving others in hard situations and giving beyond what's easy. These are important life and character lessons, and the earlier your kids learn them, the better.

Invest some thought and care in dealing with the needs of three generations. As the father, lead the way in attitude and action. If you make it a joy and a privilege to meet the demands of the people you love, both old and young, your kids will follow you.

58.

Encourage Sports Within Limits

Involvement in athletic programs, community sports activities, and family interests such as golf, skiing, and tennis adds healthy, character-building elements to the life of a growing child. As a father, your encouragement and support mean a lot. Your interest in practicing with your child, attending games and meets, or even simply being available to do some chauffeuring or coaching can make the enterprise all the more successful for your child, and a boost to your lifelong relationship together.

You may, however, observe your child's performance in organized sports with dismay. Your child is consistently the daisy-picker on the soccer field, or shows little interest during tennis lessons. You may be tempted to push for more discipline and an ever-higher level of excellence. This is fine, within limits.

A growing body of medical evidence exists illustrating the negative impact an extreme involvement in sports can have on children's development. Children who exercise too much disrupt their hormonal balance, change natural development patterns, and sometimes actually inhibit growth. Furthermore, the hardest-driving programs—with their relentless emphasis on body shape, size, and fat-to-muscle ratio—have led some kids into eating disorders and others into the use of steroids and other drugs. Instead of learning self-discipline and building social skills, they're destroying their future health and developing what may be lifelong psychological problems.

You're the adult in the situation—the one with perspective and wisdom to offer. Encourage your kids to get involved in sports at a wholesome, well-balanced level. It'll keep the fun and benefits at the forefront, and the excesses at bay.

59.

Nurture Rebellion

Rebellion is a part of growing up. It begins in early childhood, the first time a baby says "no" to Mom and Dad. We patiently respond at that stage and hide our smiles, but this is only a first step in a process that will continue until the child is independent.

The difference between a baby's "no" and an adolescent's "why?" is one of self-consciousness. Adolescents are becoming adults, and are learning to think for themselves. They have an adult's cognitive ability, minus knowledge and experience. They question whether societal norms and family norms are their norms. They ask, "Who am I?" and wonder whether Dad's rules and codes of conduct will be theirs, or if they will discover another set.

These days, our children are expected to forge their identities from an almost boundless set of opportunities and options. The task is daunting and intimidating, as well as exhilarating. They worry: "What if I choose wrong? My whole life could be determined by the choices I make now." So they experiment and test the waters.

Rebellion within bounds is good. Certainly, it's frustrating for parents, and it can escalate to frightening extremes. But the normal rebellious actions call for patience, not confrontation. Behavioral rebellion can be trying: "Okay, so I did sneak out with my friend and go to a party when you thought we were sound asleep, but it was no big deal." Depending on the extremes and outcomes, many rebellious activities are a normal part of growing up, and ought not to be unnecessarily blown out of proportion.

By giving your children space to rebel with little things, you allow them to vent enough steam to make really large eruptions unnecessary. This, of course, begs the question: "How do I know normal rebellion from extreme rebellion?" Part of the answer, of course, is the society around you. Adolescents, unlike babies, interact frequently in a larger world. If they act out in ways that are uncivil or illegal, society will let them (and you) know in no uncertain terms. But a larger answer to the question is that you need to know your children. Know their habits, their friends, their weaknesses, and their strengths. Destructive behavior needs to be curbed. Harmless rebellion needs a gentler, albeit firm, hand. Alongside all of this, when tempers are frayed and patience is worn, remember your youth and don't fear the old adage that "the apple doesn't fall far from the tree."

60.

Handle Discipline as a Team

There are many different forms of discipline, but social scientists distinguish two major categories: "guilt," where laws are established and penalties fixed in advance, not unlike a court of law today; and "shame," where the more psychological penalties of ostracism or the "silent treatment" are employed. Entire cultures are sometimes distinguished according to their overall orientation toward guilt or shame. Thus, for example, early American colonists such as the Puritans were guilt-oriented, while the Native Americans around them were more shame-oriented. In both cases, there was a consensus regarding the appropriate response to inappropriate behavior.

There is no ultimate manual of child-rearing that can enumerate every offense and specify penalties for each, nor is there any rulebook that says that a guilt philosophy should prevail over a shame philosophy. Each mom and dad must determine these matters for themselves, according to their own code of conduct and their own philosophy of child-rearing. In this regard, remember: It's not enough that you know what you want and intend to do about discipline. You and their mom are a team, and you need to act like one. When the time comes, you need to stick to your guns together, despite all of the tears and entreaties from the kids. Whatever your basic philosophy, you need to be in cahoots, and make sure that your children understand it well. Consistency is essential.

By disciplining together around a common philosophy, whatever that may be, you can ensure that handling your children's behavior will teach effectively and not simply be a brute emotional response. This, in turn, means that when applying discipline, you respond with control. It may be easier to stay the course while you're still angry—in calmer moments, nobody likes to discipline and be the bad guy—but raging anger clouds judgment and leads to excesses. If you agree that discipline is necessary, then knowing how and in what frame of mind to do it is extremely important.

Beware of your soft spots. Make no mistake that at some level, your children know you as well as you know them. They may not have your skills or your people smarts, but they know how to get to you. Hopefully, partnering with their mom in this business will allow one or the other to prevail when the temptation arises to be soft.

In discipline, as in every other aspect of parenting, parents need to be partners. Your life will be simpler, your children will be more secure, and your job as Dad will be more satisfying.

61.

Know When to Let Go

Do you remember the first time your parents let you cross the street on your bike? Chances are that they did not come to this decision easily. Lying behind that momentous decision was a lifetime of observation and careful monitoring that freed them to say, "Okay, you're ready. Off you go."

There is nothing more gratifying and frightening in parenting than removing the limits and letting children go. At first, restraints are everywhere. At infancy, your children are totally dependent and impotent. They grow into toddlers who have almost complete dependence—they can get into real trouble if they're not closely monitored at every point.

Years of close monitoring inculcate useful habits that no doubt save children's lives. But the time comes when a kid needs some breathing room to practice skills and gain self-confidence and self-sufficiency. The line between irresponsible oversight and responsible letting go is a thin one, and perhaps parents would be wise to err on the side of caution. In any case, they must be prepared to see their children cross it eventually.

As a dad, you need to be attuned to your children's development and be prepared to cut them some slack. Sometimes they will indeed bite off more than they can chew, and you'll need to put the restraints back into play. There's a negotiation here between freedom and responsibility, and you'll have to endure some tests.

In fact, the rule of thumb in letting go is constant experimentation. At each step, your children must prove themselves responsible to exercise the new freedom given. Children are all unique in how much freedom they can responsibly exercise, and when. Siblings can and do vary widely in rates of maturation and responsibility, so even within families, no generalization will tell you when to permit more freedom, and when to say, "Not yet."

When you do let go, it is a validation not only of your children's growing maturity, but also of your own confidence in your ability as a parent. To know when to let go, you have to know your children. Think about it.

62.

Remember that College
Isn't for Everyone

Education—in particular, public education—has long been a distinguished entitlement in American society. Today, we have a higher education system that is the envy of the world, attracting students from around the globe. In theory, every American child can gain access to this rich entitlement.

It's no wonder, then, that parents emphasize the virtues and accessibility of a college education to their children. They point to statistics indicating higher salary earnings and the philosophical advantages of a liberal education. Much of this is good and worthy of your children's ambition. But we've become so obsessed with what a college education can do for us that we've upped the ante. It's not enough to have a college education; for many of us, it must be the best college. If admission to an elite institution is not attained, then someone has failed.

The truth is that college isn't for everyone, and dads should beware trying to pour their children into molds that were never meant for them. Some children simply don't have the right aptitude for abstract learning. Others have the aptitude, but not the discipline and interest to sit and study for long hours. On the other hand, they may have great aptitude for crafts or mechanics or electrical work that would take them far in a trade career of their choice. You need to know your children well enough to let go of the idea of college, if appropriate. You need to allow your children to be who they are.

Similar cautions apply to college selection. Many parents are easily seduced by their children's advisors to select the finest schools that will admit them, even when the price tag is one that parents really can't afford. College tuition is one of the few expenses that has consistently outpaced inflation. You have the right to say to your children, "No matter where you're admitted, this is as much as we can afford, and no more." You are not obliged to run yourself into a perilous financial situation and unwanted debt simply because an expensive school says to your kid, "We'll take you."

Some kids may realize in high school or after their first year of college—when they have nearly flunked out—that they have the aptitude for college but not the focus or desire. Don't consider failing grades to be the end of the world, but let them serve as cause for proactive decisions. For unprepared children, college may be in the future, but not directly out of high school. With more and more "late starters" entering the ranks of colleges, the higher education system no longer consists solely of students who are unmarried and between eighteen and twenty-one. For some late bloomers, the military may be an important outlet, both as a maturing influence and as a financial resource for higher education after their service.

In the final analysis, let your children be their own individuals. Give children choices, and you and your kids will save your strength for the really important things in life.

63.

Say Goodbye Together

Rare is the child who does not experience the loss of a loved one during the course of growing up. Sometimes it's a grandparent, or even a great-grandparent, who has lived a long and fruitful life, and whose memory will live on without hurt or bitterness. But sometimes it's much closer to home: a mother, a sibling, or a childhood friend who died early in life.

What's a dad to do in these sorrowful times? Of course, every death is unique, and no stock response or set of words will fit all occasions. Indeed, that's the point. To be effective in times of loss, you must be open and vulnerable. It's not a time to hide your feelings. Neither is it a time to manufacture them if they're not there. Some men simply cannot cry at the funeral of a loved one, no matter how deep the attachment or sense of loss. These same dads may bawl like babies at the death of a pet dog. That doesn't mean the dog is more important than the loved one—only that emotions are complex. Do what comes naturally in terms of your behavior, but make a point of emotional honesty in relation to your kids.

Showing your children your vulnerability is a brave and invaluable example for them. Men grieve. The more that they shared with a loved one and the closer their relationship, the deeper the grief. Children also need to grieve. They need to know that it's okay and learn how to do it. Death is not a long vacation from the deceased, but real loss and separation. Like love, your grief needs to be shared. In grieving with your kids, you communicate that they are important and cherished, that you care for them no less because you grieve the loss of another, and that they are participants in this important facet of life.

Almost invariably, death also prompts fears of death and mortality on the part of the child. You need to let your children know that they should not fear death with any obsessive, day-to-day preoccupation. Death is a natural part of life and of life's cycle. It is a certainty, and it is mysterious, but it does not need to be terrifying. If you are religious, a death can provide an important opportunity to share your faith and its teachings on what happens during and after death. If you do not believe this, you may choose to let a death provide an opportunity to think of all that was good and noble in the life of the deceased and all that lives on in those left behind.

Death is part of our reality—but life goes on, and memories need not die. You are your children's first, best teacher, in grief, as well as joy. Let them know you well enough in the midst of grief to be encouraged and taught.

64.

Abide No Bullies

Bullying in healthy, functional families tends to take place among siblings, and here, you have to be an ever-vigilant and careful referee. Keep in mind that older sisters are as prone to being bullies as older brothers. The only difference is that eventually, the younger siblings catch up to their older sisters and impose some sort of equality. Also, in early years, younger boys are as vulnerable to abuse as girls are. So assume nothing about who is at fault.

Often, bullying will take place out of your sight, but signs will be there if you have eyes to see them. The clearest signal comes when the victims tell you what is happening. But sometimes the intimidation is so great that they don't. You need to be a close observer of the interpersonal dynamics among your children and alert to telltale signs such as flinches, mysterious bruises and scrapes, or even downright hatred. Sometimes younger siblings seem to "ask for it" if they begin whining or crying. Explain and show that crying, which is typical of a certain age group, must not be addressed with physical abuse.

While we typically associate bullies with the schoolyard, it is important to remember that schools are not usually the training grounds of bullies. These habits are learned in the home. You have the position and the clout to put an end to this sort of behavior before it becomes a problem.

65.

Know Their Friends

When our children are young, we take great care to protect them wherever they go. They play in our company, talk in our company, and argue in our company. On occasions when our friends or family members take responsibility for them, we assume commonalties and safety. But as our children become older, they also become more elusive. Schools, sports, bikes, clubs, sleepovers, and chauffeuring parents bring them into ever-larger circles of association with children that you may not know. Eventually, there's dating and becoming couples, again in circles that may be strange to us.

Your kids' friends and peer groups play a strong role in shaping values and personality. You ignore them at your peril. You won't like everything about your children's friends, but don't stress about that. No friend of your child could ever match up to all the qualities you might attach to the ideal friend: being kind, attentive, challenging, helpful, always sympathetic, and never mean or self-centered. Children will be children, and you'll find out in a hurry that your children don't have a monopoly on selfishness, immaturity, or meanness.

But sometimes your children's friends can be corrosive, or even destructive of values and behavior you know to be wholesome and just. Perhaps they encourage bullying; maybe it's stealing, drugs, or bigotry. When you tune in to associations such as these, monitor them closely, and if necessary, terminate them. Under extreme circumstances, it may even be necessary to change neighborhoods or schools to break up destructive associations. It's worth it.

The only way to separate the small flaws in imperfect friends from the major problems in unacceptable friends is to *know* your children's friends. Make an effort to observe them. Chat for a moment when they phone before calling your child to pick up. This will give you an impression, though incomplete and perhaps misleading. From an early age, talk to your children about their friends. Ask about brothers, sisters, mothers, and fathers. Does their friend's dad or mom have a nickname? Where do the parents work? Vacation? Dine? Give your children and their friends the benefit of the doubt so that they won't clam up from fear of judgment. If you cultivate this habit of nonjudgmental curiosity and interest in their lives, they will not find ongoing interest and curiosity as alienating during adolescence.

When it comes to dating, you have a right to ask pointed questions and to meet any dates. Face-to-face meetings can give a lot of information at first impression, but they need to be followed up by questions. Again, curiosity is more effective than confrontation.

Fathers of boys need to know whom their sons are dating as much as those of girls. Good and bad choices go both ways. The more you know about your children's friends, the more you can enjoy your parenting job while they're with you.

66.

Don't Make Allowance a Gift

It's Saturday morning, and to many kids, that means allowance time. This is a happy moment for children, but dads might want to think twice about what it means. In fact, giving an allowance offers wonderful opportunities to teach lessons about earning money and money management that will pay lasting dividends beyond what any bank might offer.

Children learn money management skills at home to a far greater extent than you might imagine. For starters, they are watching you and their mother. Rare is the parent who can sequester all financial discussions from children's eager ears, and that's probably good. In hearing the discussions, they learn that money is not limitless. In fact, your resources must be managed responsibly, both for your own sake and the sake of your family. In money matters such as taxes or social security, your children should learn how their government is supported, and what it means in old age or joblessness.

Equally important are the lessons that children learn from managing their own allowance. You may wish to tie allowance directly to weekly chores so that your children learn the connection between work and compensation, or alternatively, the failure to work and the withholding of compensation. Whether earned or not, children learn money management through the sheer act of spending their allowance. Inevitably, your children will have experiences in which they use their allowance and then desperately want money for some unanticipated pleasure. You can choose to "advance" the needed money, thus teaching borrowing and lending. You might want to devise additional chores that can generate additional money, teaching the value of "overtime." Or you might want to tell your kids that they have to wait until next week, teaching the value of budgeting. In any case, your kids learn the unforgettable lesson that money isn't free, but comes with a set of rules and expectations. Let them know that such rules govern the economic lives of everyone, from children to parents and poor to rich.

Other forms of work and savings can supplement weekly allowance. For example, you may want to have your children begin a holiday account whereby they deposit a certain portion of their allowance into a savings account that can be withdrawn on the eve of the holidays for gift purchases. You may also wish to encourage your kids to withhold a portion of their allowance for giving to good causes, teaching the lesson of charity and giving.

Think of yourself as a financial schoolhouse. If the buck doesn't stop with you on the education side, it will be begged from you on the spending side, and you'll be faced with stresses that you won't enjoy.

67.

Organize Your Neighborhood

In this era of after-school activities, camps, sports, and clubs, it's easy to forget that your children live in a neighborhood and participate in a unique circle of association that isn't defined by ages, grades, or gender. On a hot summer day with nothing to do, it's amazing how many different age groups of both genders can come together and invent their fun. You can help in this process, especially during after-school hours or summer evenings.

Don't worry that your kids will resent your jumping into their business. In fact, such responses are rare. Making yourself part of the playing, especially by organizing games and events, is an important role that tells your children (and others) that the child inside us doesn't disappear with adulthood. Every good neighborhood has parents who dare to get involved with their neighbors' children and their friends. Some build tree houses, some host basketball or soccer, and others spearhead trips to go ice skating on Saturday afternoons.

Club sports, music groups, and school plays are important—but we live our lives in a local community. Sociologists have long contrasted impersonal and autonomous "society" from caring, mutually supportive "community." Where society alienates and depersonalizes, community affirms and brings together. Don't let your neighborhood become a society for you or your children. Build community where it begins, around and between you and your neighbors. You'll create an atmosphere in which pettiness gives way to camaraderie and support.

68.

Make Chores a Team Effort

Whether chores are tied to allowances or simply defined as part of what being a family member is all about, they are far more important than the actual jobs being performed. Rare is the person who can go through life without having to earn a living, and it is never too early to shape attitudes toward work.

For starters, you may need to ask what work means to you. Is it simply a burden, an unpleasant tour of duty which is better ended sooner than later? Or do you find some intrinsic rewards in work that serve your sense of well-being and self-esteem? For most dads, the latter is the real answer. Truth be told, you would be lost if you didn't have work. Work defines the parameters of your weeks and gives meaning to your "days of rest."

In assigning chores, work with your children. At home, families have a common goal—a functioning, cooperative household—and they have a set of discrete tasks that need to be divided. Initially, the contributions of the youngest child will be minimal. Perhaps they will amount to nothing more than being responsible for keeping a room clean. But through even minimal chores, children learn that they are essential to the team. Work supplements words and affection in building a sense of security and belonging.

When assigning tasks, keep in mind each child's limitations. Nothing is more discouraging to a child than to have you measure tasks according to your own time frame. A lawn that takes you one hour to rake may well take a child three hours. By keeping kids' limitations in mind, you will avoid underestimating jobs and building resentment.

Effective business managers have learned that by instilling a sense of team play and insisting that all players have contributions to make, the organization inherits the rich rewards of creative ideas from the bottom up. There's a lesson here for family chores, as well. Children who are kept in the consulting loop feel like they are a part of household "management." Perhaps they will discover alternative chores that hadn't occurred to you that give their lives special meaning. By letting your children help define their chores while keeping the needs of the larger team in mind, you give them a sense of power and build their ability to be future leaders themselves.

Make chores a valued part of your family's life, not a burden. Don't even call them chores. Call them "house activities" or something else that suggests that the team is about to get busy. Ensure that the shared labor of living at home doesn't become the source of stress and strife.

69.

Eat Sensibly

We now know that eating disorders in this country are approaching epidemic proportions. We know that these disorders can go to extremes and be fatal for our children. Dads need to understand this grim *fact—really* understand it. Malnutrition is not a third-world problem; it's an American problem, and it's getting worse every year. What's a father to do?

First, be very serious about the subject of food and nutrition. Health classes in school will not be enough if you're not practicing what you preach. In many households, the mother tends to do the food shopping and cooking. As a result, you may feel unimportant to your kids' eating habits. But don't be deceived. Whether you like it or not, you are a role model in this, as in all arenas of life. If you're a couch potato, addicted to fatty foods and frequent TV snacks, your children will learn the habit. They will interpret such eating as part of the entertainment and fun of life. If you have that bag of potato chips every evening, so will your children. Eating junk food and taking a cavalier attitude about the health effects of your food choices may be a message your kids will follow all too easily when they're on their own.

Eating is social, as well as biological, and conversation is often at its best and most effective over a good meal. There is no better time to bring behavior and talk together. What you say to your family about nutrition and the food you're eating is important. Relish good food, and talk about what makes it good. Encourage your children to connect good eating habits with health. Don't let any false impressions from the media stand without frequent comment.

Put your mouth where your money is. In the final analysis, we are what we eat. Show your kids a wholesome approach to food, and make meals together a time for learning who your children are and who they want to be.

70.

Remember the Arts

The signs are everywhere today: "Do Sports, Not Drugs." While this is good advice, it can be restraining. Not all kids are interested in sports. The idea that children need to be encouraged to pursue activities that are wholesome and involving is a sound one, but your kids may simply not be sports types.

Parents, and sports-minded dads in particular, need to keep other creative and recreational signs in their parenting toolkit: "Do Art, Not Drugs," "Do Music, Not Drugs," "Do Drama, Not Drugs," "Do Poetry, Not Drugs," and so on. Unlike most team sports, the arts provide lifelong pursuits that have proven to be a powerful, effective alternative to the sports scene for many children. A child may not have a future as a world-class artist, any more than all young athletes are future pros, but all children have some area of interest and ability that they can pursue. Your responsibility is to provide access and exposure to enough different arts that your children have ample opportunity to discover whether creative connections capture their interest and energy.

Schedule regular times to take your kids to art exhibits, concerts, and plays. If they show literary interests, buy books instead of games. Get them involved in choosing what you'll do together, and look for options the kids can relate to in some way. Obviously, forcing them to go to a concert on a sunny Saturday afternoon when all the other kids are outside playing may well produce unwanted consequences. Find a time when an outing is natural and can even include extended family or friends. Make it fun.

Work to get your children involved in the areas of the arts that they show interest in. Look for community arts shops and drama workshops. If your kids like music, then consider professional lessons. Once commitments are made and dollars have been paid out, you have the right to insist on follow-through, even if it's only for a season. Artistic recreation, no less than athletic recreation, requires self-discipline that in itself teaches lessons for life. The difference between individual artistic expression and team sports is that if your children decide to pursue the arts, you get to be the coach at home and make sure practice happens regularly.

Finally, make your household a place where the arts thrive. Let there be music and literature. Make way for the mess that often accompanies artistic expression. Even if art is the furthest thing from your mind in terms of personal interest, make provision for the work of local artists or tune in to dramatic presentations. These need not be of professional quality and they need not be expensive. The only requirement is letting artistic imagination have its place.

71.

Tell the Truth, but
Not the Whole Truth

Before we testify in court, we swear to tell "the truth, the whole truth, and nothing but the truth." This oath is crucial to a rule of law, and is the means by which strangers are brought together on a trustworthy foundation. But homes are not courts, and children are not district attorneys pressing us to tell the whole truth in a world of strangers. Sometimes a less-than-whole truth is the wiser course of parenting.

Take adolescence, for example. Virtually every child goes through an awkward stage. Sometimes the awkwardness is due to a gangling body not yet filled in, or a pudgy body not quite shed of baby fat. Sometimes it's from thick glasses, or braces, or acne. This is one of the most painful periods in a child's life, and one fraught with uncertainty and insecurity. Your child may well say, "Dad, I'm pretty ugly, aren't I?" or, "Dad, I'm never going to have a date. Who'd want to go out with *me?*" What do you say?

Common sense as a parent urges circumspection. While no child will be satisfied with a bald-faced lie, you need to be extremely cautious and sensitive. Your words matter deeply, and even the slightest nuance can be picked up and never forgotten. Dads can never repeat too often such words as, "You're beautiful," or "You're getting strong."

Don't let your children, in their despair, get you to go along with their transitional insecurities. See the big picture that they cannot see in their own self-absorbed and immediate state. That big picture takes into account the remarkable changes that occur once puberty is breached. The picture should indeed be beautiful to you, someone who knows and loves them deeply. Your children need to hear the real "whole truth" from you.

72.

Limit the Damage

What parent hasn't been embarrassed by something their child has done in a public place? The baby wails endlessly in a restaurant; the twelve-year-old insists on a loud debate with parents or siblings; the teenager exhibits an undreamed-of lack of manners around other adults.

Embarrassment in public places calls for a unified response from parents. It is tempting in such circumstances for Dad to take charge in a highly public way that lets onlookers know that he is a better disciplinarian and parent than his children's inappropriate behavior might suggest. But this runs the risk of alienating Mom, or worse, making an embarrassing situation even more so for everyone involved.

Embarrassing public behavior calls for an immediate response, but not necessarily a public response. A wailing baby in a restaurant can be carried out of the dining area. If Mom is more often at home with the baby than Dad is, it's not only loving but also fair that Dad give Mom a break by taking the baby outside. If all else fails, call it a night and head for home. The baby probably needs to be in bed.

The kids that can't get along in public need a walk away from others and some ground rules. Even better, set up the rules in advance: "This is how we behave when we go out," followed by very specific repercussions for noncompliance. There's nothing wrong with asking, "Can I count on you for this, or do you need to stay home?" Once they buy in, you've got them. Consistent discipline for misbehavior will make repeat performances unlikely.

Of course, adolescent rebellion loves a public space. On some level, kids think, "I've got you. I can act out here, and you won't make a scene." Your children have to learn that indeed you won't make a scene, but neither have they succeeded in exploiting the moment for rebellion against you. A quiet but stern word may stem the tide. If that fails and your teen is bound and determined to make everyone miserable, you and your wife together may make an executive decision to cut your losses and run. Simply terminate the meal, concert, or reception and leave. Along the way, let your kids know that you are perfectly happy to try again, but that it must be the real children and not the rebels who show up. With three strikes, they are "out" of chances to go places for a period of time. When everyone knows the rules, it takes much of the stress out of dealing with the problem.

73.

Take Them One at a Time

Parents soon discover that their children are as different from one another as they themselves are different from each other. Out of two combined gene pools emerge myriad permutations that make each child unique and uniquely lovable. Some children are more outgoing and demonstrative, while others are introspective and shy. This presents both delights and challenges for the average dad.

Don't let the external characteristics of your children's personalities dictate the amount of quality time and attention that they receive. You'll often hear it said that this child or that "demands more attention," but this is not really accurate. Every child requires attention in the form of concern, love, interest, and relationship. They just don't all express it equally. Give demanding children their due, and be thankful that they remind you of their needs. But be careful not to neglect the quiet children, who need you just as much, if not more.

You may find that you have other challenges related to giving equal attention to your children. First, resist the temptation to concentrate more attention on your son(s) than your daughter(s).

The old stereotype of Dad playing catch with his son while his daughter plays with her dolls in the kitchen with Mom is outdated and contrived. You can—and should—play sports with your daughters no less than your sons, if that's where their interests lie. Beyond that, you'll provide your daughters with a measure of self-confidence and ease in the presence of adult males that will carry over into their adult lives.

Take care, as well, never to hold up one child in comparison with another. It's fine for you to encourage competitive games among your children in which one will win and the others lose. It gives you the opportunity to teach good sportsmanship at close range. But asking one child, for example, why a report card isn't as strong as a sibling's, or why one child can't always be cheery the way the other is, creates destructive patterns. It sets up resentments, a negative self-image, and a sense of unworthiness that may follow the child for life. You may not be able to avoid the observations. Just keep them to yourself.

Positive comparisons with siblings, on the other hand, can be powerfully reinforcing. To say that a son is kind, just like his older sister, or that your daughter has her older brother's skill in math, provides a sense of family identity and cohesion that is good. In fact, you may find that the kids follow your lead and become mutually reinforcing of one another's strengths.

Every child is a one-of-a-kind masterpiece. If you convey that message in your interactions with them, they'll have good footing on which to build positive, meaningful lives.

74.

Create the Great Adventures

If you had a happy childhood, chances are that you still recall a number of great adventures in which your father played a central role. Perhaps it's a trip to the ocean or the amusement park, or a cross-country car tour of interesting and fun places. These are the high points of growing up, and they remind you of how central your family—and father—were to your growing up.

Great adventures often require time, planning, and money. Because of this, realistically, these adventures occur infrequently in the lives of most families. But don't let that stop you from taking every opportunity to make even the most mundane activity or rainiest day a call for some kind of plan. Every child has a built-in sense of adventure that needs only to be tapped to come alive. Kids can create adventures in their own imaginations by simply reading a good book, watching a good movie, or just playing alone in the backyard.

Adventures with you are a different matter. As Dad, you must come up with adventures that will work for both of you. This requires a more creative mindset. How can you make car washing an adventure? What can you imagine as you walk together on an unfamiliar path? How can walking or running together become a challenge?

Creating adventures is as easy as telling stories, with you as the lead storyteller and the kids following up and adding their own chapters. Adventures are a time for heroism together. In the world of fantasy, you and your children have the opportunity to overcome obstacles and share in the achievement.

Every day holds the potential for an adventure, but don't forget the big ones. If you're planning a family cross-country tour, bring your children into the planning. Study maps together and plan sights that you all would like to see. Encourage grandparents and other family members to become partners in the fun.

You may have lost your own sense of adventure beneath the burdens of daily life. Let your kids and your imagination show you the way back.

75.

Be a Man

As a child, how many times did you hear, "Grow up and be a man"? While most dads heard that frequently in their youth, they probably had little idea exactly what it meant. For many, being a man implied being insensitive, not only to pain, but also to emotion; it meant never admitting weakness or vulnerability. Today, boys hear "you're the man" when they score a point in a game. Yet none of these is what being a man is all about.

Being a man has little to do with heroic talk and bragging. As a dad, you won't teach your children about manliness with words. You'll *do* it. Courtesy, civility, and helping the weak are certainly near the top of anyone's list of what it means to be a man. But these are things for women to practice, as well, and might more properly come under the label of "being a caring adult." Is there anything distinctive about being a man that is not chauvinistic or sexist? There most emphatically is, and it begins with simply taking pride in your gender. Understanding that you're a man can and should make you glad.

You are typically physically stronger than women or children. With that physical strength comes responsibility to protect in danger, be careful during physical interaction, and restrain impulses when someone says to stop. You are also part of a society that has taken its good time in affording women equal rights and opportunities. Many discriminatory situations continue, in which men are privileged over their female counterparts. You'll show what you're made of as a man when you make a point of redressing these inequities in your practices, attitudes, and conversation.

Taking pride in your gender also means taking pride in primary associations with other men in your life. Male associations need not be elitist or discriminatory. A men's golf group, card game, or meditation group is appropriate and worth cultivating.

It has been observed that men are taught to be so competitive that they usually don't make close male friends beyond their college years. Ask them who their closest friends are, and in contrast to many women, they will invoke distant friendships from years gone by. This is unfortunate and worth challenging. Seek close friends among your male associations, and together, "be the men" for your children and their generation.

76.

Take a Breather

Even the most devoted dad gets shopworn from time to time. Kids demand a lot of attention and take a lot of energy, not to mention patience, endurance, and wisdom. Parenting can leave you with frayed nerves and a short fuse. You may feel as if you travel from one set of responsibilities (at home) to the next (at work) to the next (back at home). It can leave you weary, stressed, and dissatisfied.

If this is you, it's time for a break. Being a father does not mean that you have to give up on being you. If you have hobbies that refresh you, keep them alive. If you have a group of friends with whom you share interests, find ways that you can continue to build and sustain those relationships. If what you enjoy more than anything is a getaway with your wife, make the necessary arrangements and go away together regularly—at least once a year.

You may have to make adjustments. The time and flexibility you enjoyed as a single man is no longer an option. And the way you did things when you and your wife did not have kids is not likely to be replicated on a regular basis until the chicks are out of the nest. Among other things, you'll need your wife's support and cooperation to make sure your breathers are stress-relievers instead of stress-producers. In fact, she might enjoy some breathers of her own. Offering equal time for her to play while *you* watch the kids and keep the household running is a great way to give both of you a shot of renewed energy and enthusiasm for the hard work of raising kids.

Create opportunities to "play" with the grown-ups, and let your children miss you for a short spell. They'll be fine, and you'll be a better dad because you'll be whole and refreshed.

77.

Give Pets Their Due

Most children will live to see their pets die. For some children, this may prove to be a more traumatic loss in their lives than that of a distant grandparent, for example. This is especially true in the event of children witnessing the death of a pet, whether accidental or after a long illness. Unlike human beings, most pets die at home or on the highway. This means that the experience will be more direct and visceral than most human losses.

In death as in life, pets are an important learning experience for your children. They represent opportunities for shared grieving and coping with loss. You need to be sensitive to the emotions of your children. There may be immediate reactions, delayed reactions, or both. In any case, your emotional antennae have to be up and your willingness to sympathize has to be constant.

You may think to compensate for the loss of a pet by getting a replacement pet as soon as possible. This may or may not be appropriate to your situation. But don't act simply to quell your child's immediate loss. Sometimes coping with loss for an appropriate period is as important as moving beyond it. With your presence and compassion, your child will learn and grow through the experience.

78.

Be Your Children's Best Teacher

If and when bad grades arrive home from school, you will never be more important in your role as home teacher. How you respond will be crucial to your relationship with your children, because you will speak volumes to them about a difficult situation. This is a moment of childhood "failure"—one you can be sure that your child feels. Reflexive, angry discipline or fawning comforting that is blind to the reality of poor performance represent the extreme reactions. Somewhere between them falls the balanced, calm, and deliberate response of a wise father.

Like all successful teachers, you need to think in terms of a teacher's plan for every learning experience in your children's lives, including poor grades. For starters, don't be surprised by bad grades. Some kids tend to be unrealistically optimistic about their performance in school, while others lean toward being unrealistically pessimistic. In either case, you can't afford to be so fooled by their self-assessment that you'll be surprised by a less than sterling outcome.

Poor school performance happens for reasons, and you'll need to zero in on those if you want to facilitate improvement in your child's grades. This doesn't require anger; in fact, it's hampered by anger, because your ire can effectively put your child on the defensive, leading nowhere. Sometimes poor performance in a subject is a simple lack of competence that no amount of pressure or punishment will ever correct. Tutoring may help, but within a limited horizon that must be faced and accepted. Not every child is destined to be a rocket scientist. At the other extreme, poor performance may be a simple product of boredom on the part of an exceptionally competent student. Lacking sufficient stimulation in the classroom, the child daydreams and discovers other more creative outlets for abilities. This, too, requires an appropriate response, certainly in consultation with the school, to provide the challenge that will better motivate your child.

Sometimes bad grades reflect a behavioral problem grounded in physical or emotional causes. Active children often have difficulty sitting still, particularly in early years. They may be "high-strung," with energy to burn. At other times—particularly when bad grades appear out of the blue—you may discover more emotional causes grounded in recent events that call for professional counseling.

In all of these scenarios, you'll do well to begin by talking to the teachers evaluating your child. Once children are in school, their teachers often know more about them than their parents. Any good teacher will value your desire to consult, and will often prove surprisingly adept at suggesting strategies and possibilities. On the other hand, you also know your child, and shouldn't be afraid to question a teacher's judgment or assessment.

By the time your kids are teenagers, your inclination to overreact can be overwhelming. You know that classroom performance in high school can in many ways establish the educational and vocational destiny of your child. You may care more than your child, even care too much, and for the wrong reasons. Grades are important—a wakeup call—but they aren't life and death.

Whatever the cause of bad grades, you cannot escape the obligation to invest time in the problem. Professional teachers do not displace or replace fathers. When grades turn poor, don't go off the deep end. Get busy.

79.

Get Them Dressed Up

Kids predictably get caught up in the latest fads of dress and style for their age groups and their era. It's as old as community—people living and working together—and it tends to be harmless. Yet we all recognize that dressing properly for certain occasions plays an influential part in living in a civil society and presenting ourselves to others.

What do we teach our children about dress, and beyond that, manners and sociability? Begin with how you and your wife dress and carry yourself. Your children will observe you as you leave for work, return home for relaxation, and go out on the weekend. You probably do not wear the same shirt and pants multiple days in a row; you dress differently on the weekends than during the week; and you get dressed up for special occasions. In all of these examples, you show respect for the occasion at hand by your choices.

The respect you teach your children to show in how they dress has its natural extension in their manners and comportment. This includes everything from a firm handshake and looking the other person in the eye, to easy greetings instead of mumbled phrases with head down and eyes averted. It includes consideration for the elderly and physically challenged, politeness to people who are serving you, and holding open a door for those behind you.

A casualty of public school education has been instruction on manners and dress. Quite simply, there is no consensus about proper dress or even behavior. Consequently, you and your wife *are* the school of manners for your children. Whatever particular code of behavior you prefer for your children, some underlying principles exist. Chief among them are courtesy, modesty, and respect for others. These principles first reveal themselves to others in the way we dress.

Clearly, there is more to dressing up than pomp and circumstance. As you conduct yourself, you model for your children the rules that a civil society depends on. This has little to do with trends. It has everything to do with what we say about ourselves by our presentation. Teach them well on this subject. Let them know that there are times and places for a variety of styles; it's not a free-for-all if they want their appearance to communicate something about them. The trendy stuff may be fine in their kid world. In other settings, it may not. Teach them how to get dressed up. The impact on their lives is real and lasting.

80.

Temper, Temper

Some people never learn to control their tempers. If asked, most of us can rattle off a list of adults that we know with legendary tempers. Many of these people have suffered grievously as a result. Colleagues don't wish to work with them, friends grow alienated, spouses leave them, and success in life passes them by.

How we respond as parents to our children's tempers has long-term consequences for their lives. As counterintuitive as it may sound, your best bet is not to stress about the early temper tantrums excessively. Most kids have them. Shows of temper are less cause for concern than they are teaching opportunities.

As a dad, you begin teaching temper control by example. Just as everyone knows people who lose their tempers, most families can recall moments when a mom or dad "lost it" in a situation that later—perhaps much later—appears funny. The humor is possible because the tantrum was unusual. But if one or both parents are constantly losing their temper, the family finds little to laugh about.

The line between rage and violence is thin, and holds everyone hostage to its implied threat. When you control your temper in stressful situations, you not only exhibit an important lesson, but you set your children's minds and nervous systems at ease.

If you see increasing temper tantrums in your children over the years, or if you observe dramatic or explosive sorts of rage, the temper itself and not what causes it should be your first concern. The cause of an exploding temper is often less serious and troubling to perceptive parents than the need for temper management. Address it directly, and if need be, seek some professional help. Don't let it go.

For most people, self-control represents a learning curve over a lifetime. New and unanticipated stresses and frustrations always arise that call for relearning the practice of self-control. By staying on that learning curve yourself, you can go a long way in teaching your children to do the same.

81.

Put Limits on Your Work Life

Many fathers complain regularly about work, and speak longingly about the weekend and retirement. But this isn't necessarily truthful. For many dads, work is home away from home, and quite fulfilling. Despite pressure, frustrations with coworkers, and bad bosses, work often represents productivity and achievement, collegiality, and team spirit. Not least, work represents money and all that money can provide. Money is often considered the adult report card, and its totals bring A's, B's, or C's. Providing for a family can be wonderfully rewarding and satisfying as a husband and a dad. On the other hand, your loved ones provide no measurable feedback—and they're easy to neglect.

How do you put limits on your work to spend time at home? Perspective is essential. And perspective begins with commitment. Take a moment, a day, or perhaps even a weekend, alone with yourself. With no distractions or demands, answer two questions: "What are my chief commitments in life?" and "Why did I want to have children?" At the end of your life, what do you most want to say about a life well-lived—*your* life well-lived? If the answer is a big career or loads of money, then no amount of good will or hopeful talk will change where you put your effort for more than a fleeting period of time. Alternatively, if your answer has more to do with loving faithfully and having a positive impact on the lives of the people you raised, then home is more important, and work deserves less of you.

Finding perspective as both a working man and a father involves enough humility to realize that you're not indispensable to your job. Calls from your career for unlimited loyalty are inappropriate. In fact, graveyards are filled with "indispensable" people. Yet life somehow goes on. Savvy corporation presidents are realizing the same thing and freeing up their employees for greater flex time, which in most cases means more time for loved ones.

While the job can go on without you, your family cannot—at least not so as to remain an intact, balanced family. Your partner almost certainly feels an excessive burden when your work takes top billing in your life; she may even come to harbor resentments that damage your relationship. But the costs to children are even greater. An absentee dad who is unavailable simply because he has let work take over sends the painful emotional message to his children that work matters more to him than they do. All the money in the world won't restore the lost confidence and lost sense of self that absentee dads impose on their children.

Perspective is key, but action makes the difference. Do you value your family and home over all else? Prove it. At the end of your life, you'll have something to look back on with pride and satisfaction.

82.

Remember That Kids
Will Play Doctor

Sexual experimentation is part of growing up. Rare is the child who has not had some innocent, if explicit, experience with the opposite sex in a prepubescent setting. Most dads (and moms) can recall similar experiences from their own childhoods. In most cases, it is cause for neither alarm, nor guilt. The parents who discover their child "in the act" are also rare, but in the event of discovery, the wise parent backs off without creating trauma or shame.

As children grow into adolescence, it is inevitable that experimentation will continue, first through masturbation, and then through dating. Here, dads are especially important counselors to their sons and daughters. Daughters need to be taught and reminded regularly that they—and they alone—will bear the full brunt of responsibility for intercourse leading to pregnancy. It is not just gender stereotyping and sexism that brands boys the aggressors and girls the resisters. Quite simply, girls have much more at stake, and need to understand that.

Girls also need to understand something of the male psyche, which dads are uniquely positioned to offer. As they enter teenage years, girls need to know that boys have raging hormones, but that their needs cannot and should not be allowed to determine behavior in a relationship. Each father must decide for himself how explicit he wants to be, or where his own moral compass draws various lines on sexual play and dating behavior. But too much reticence and shyness on the dad's part can lead to ignorance or a confused sexual understanding on a daughter's side, and all aspects of sexual expression may be naively perceived as part of the same package; in other words, if one thing is okay, everything is. Again, such ignorance will have the most devastating ramifications for the girls.

To their sons, fathers need to reiterate that there is one absolute line in the sand that no boy or young man can cross, and that is drawn by the girl who wants to stop. At any time, at any stage of engagement, for any reason, or for no apparent reason, no means no. Stop means stop. Fathers cannot stress this too often or in terms that are too emphatic. This is an absolute, inviolable principle. Date rape is not only a crime; it's an injustice and a dishonor. Furthermore, no young man is as truly "out of control" as he may think or want to believe. Hormones can be repressed, and they must be repressed if a girl is not willing to go along. Virtually any adolescent boy is physically stronger than a girl, but that has no place in a relationship. No means no.

Underlying all of this, of course, is a more fundamental code. Only you know the values that you hold and want to impart, and it's your honor and duty to impart them. Just remember that kids of all ages will experiment with their sexuality. So while you're making ideals explicit, exercise your realism, as well. There's room for experimentation within limits—and then there's responsibility, accountability, and the potential for life-changing mistakes. All you can do is your part. Just be sure that you do it.

83.

Make Mom Your Teammate

Nothing undermines a family's happiness and effectiveness more than a divided parent team, especially when it means that one parent is siding with the kids in opposition to the other parent. Once parents openly disagree about the children in front of the children, it is almost impossible to achieve a constructive outcome. Divided parents are truly conquered parents, and no one knows this more clearly than the kids. Once witnessed, kids naturally seek to exploit the tension, either to get what they want or to avoid the full brunt of either parent's anger.

A variety of causes can lead to such parental rifts. Sometimes, at the end of a hectic day, with disappointments on all sides, a father overreacts and acts out his frustrations on his children; Mom sees it happens and wants to protect the children. Sometimes mothers and fathers have genuine differences of philosophy that point to different rules and responses. In the worst situations, parents are literally separated or divorced and give in to the temptation to side with the children in open defiance of the other—for reasons of insecurity, vindictiveness, or pain.

No matter what the circumstances or the issues, parents must struggle to keep a united front. It's a matter of maturity and responsibility. Families, like armies or sports teams, do not consist of equals among whom alliances and coalitions can change from day to day and issue to issue. Families need not (and ought not) be patriarchal in the traditional sense of male dominance and double standards. But families *are* hierarchical—a society of unequals. Parents, however loving and sensitive, are in charge. And children, destined though they are to become adults one day, are nevertheless subordinate in the household.

Socialization depends a great deal on learning the nature of hierarchy and authority. There has not been, nor ever will be, a society of equals. Implicit in social order is the concept of authority and superiority, however democratically arrived at. Without order, chaos ensues, both in the family and in the larger society. For parents to be openly divided and clashing before their kids is to upset not only the domestic economy of the household, but even more, the process of socialization that children will carry with them into the world.

So what's the solution? You need to work at making Mom your teammate-in-command, just as she needs to work at making you the same. Of course, there will be differences of opinion—sometimes *enormous* differences of opinion. These require a routine of discussions designed to take place behind the scenes. The greater the issue, or the more extreme the estrangement between father and mother, the more necessary the routine. It's not necessary that your children believe you never disagree, but it is necessary that both you and your partner say, "I need to talk to you in private," when the differences arise. And children need to respect that privacy.

Children can and do derive a sense of power from dividing their parents. But it's an inappropriate power that threatens the family and, ultimately, the larger society it models. Make your spouse your teammate in parenting, and keep the disagreements private.

84.

Be the Hero, Not the Mascot

In the egalitarian age in which we live, it sounds almost anachronistic for a dad to say, "I want to be my children's hero." But there is nothing wrong with such an aspiration. The fact is that if you love and honor them, your children *will* look up to you. And as they enter adulthood, they may well look upon you as a hero in their life. Nobody except your wife is more aware of your weaknesses than your children are. But you don't have to be perfect to be a hero—real-life heroes are always real men and women. Their secret to success is not the absence of faults, but rather the capacity to transcend those faults through heart and a will that are in the right place.

Mascots are different from heroes. They are constructed in the imaginations of the children or group, and exist to serve the interests of the creator. Your children may cast you in the mascot role in a variety of ways, some overt and others subtle. In fact, this may be the context in which they try to play Dad off against Mom; they cast Dad as the gentle protector against the "grinch" (Mom) who is stealing their fun. Any normal dad longs to be loved by his children, but sometimes children play on a dad's vulnerability.

If your child says, "I don't love you anymore," or "You're not my hero," don't consider that the end of the world. You're old enough to know what a hero is really made of, and you don't have to become your children's mascot to win their love. You simply have to love them faithfully in the best way that you know how, and according to your deepest beliefs and values. If you do, the time will come when your children will also know the difference between hero and mascot, and they'll know that they got the better option in you.

85.

Take Your Kids to Work

We are all familiar with the "take your child to work" days. These provide wonderful opportunities to introduce your children to that other life that beckons you so often and seems so distant and alien. For sons and daughters, it offers the opportunity to see you in action, and maybe to say, "When I grow up, I want to do what Dad does."

In earlier times, when work and home were not separate, children constantly interacted with both parents and were integral members of the household "economy." In modern times, work and home are typically separate. But work does not have to become a source of alienation from home, or a rival to the family. By bringing your children into your world of work as often as possible (surely more than one token day per year), some of that alienation can be broken down, and children can be incorporated into your larger world.

Even when you can't bring your kids physically to work, it is important to keep thoughts of your kids with you, in the form of photos, cards, letters, and memorabilia that they've made just for you. Your work life and all that goes with it has the capacity to alienate you from your home and kids. If work becomes all-encompassing, it leaves little or no room for that other major part of your life. You lose your perspective on the home front, and cease to know your children on an intimate, instinctual level. You become the drop-in that they learn not to count on. By bringing your kids to work and keeping them with you—on your desk and on your walls—you keep home firmly on your mind and in your heart. In fact, you remember where your heart is most deeply invested. With any luck, you translate that into a steady, constructive tie to home and family.

86.

Keep the Hobby

Remember the days before the kids came on the scene? There was golf on weekends, midweek bridge or poker games with the guys, a skeet-shooting club, or a bowling league. Then you married and the kids arrived, and all of those activities seemed to melt away.

Did they have to? Raising children is arguably the most important thing that you will ever do in your lifetime, and their place in your life necessitates some inevitable changes. But as in so many areas of living with relationships, it is sometimes too easy to overcompensate and be an "all work and no play" dad, who lives only to support his family and, in the process, suppresses his own needs and pleasures.

In the long run, all work and no play turns out to be counterproductive. When you deny yourself the hobbies and activities that give lightness and joy to your weekly routines, you deny healthy outlets for adult fun that will actually make you a better father. Mothers, because of the conventional role they have

187

so often had to play, have long known how confining such a life can be. As lovable as they are, children do not make good conversation partners on an adult level; they can't share adult experiences; and they can't challenge you in a game of sport or wit. They're children. You're an adult.

Children have their just claims on you, and so does your wife. But you have just claims on yourself, as well, and to deny or suppress them with the idea that you are thus enhancing your family life is a dangerous tack to take. A life stripped clean of much-enjoyed hobbies or pastimes can lead to devastating consequences when the urge to break free turns dark. Suddenly, all of the seemingly small denials translate into a self-destructive urge to deny yourself nothing, even at the expense of your family.

Of course it's probable that you won't have quite the time for sports and hobbies that you once enjoyed, and this may mean a certain diminution of achievement and talent. If you play golf once a week, you probably won't play as well as you did when you played three times a week. Don't sweat it. If the pastimes are put in proper perspective, it's not the end result that counts, but the process of recreation, fraternization, and renewal that matters. So lighten up, Dad. You deserve your playtime. Take it.

87.

Remember God

It is for good reason that religion and politics have come to be thought of as taboo subjects in polite company. Both have the potential to become quickly divisive, even among friends, never mind the potential to start and fuel wars between clans, sects, and even nations. It's no wonder people that tend to keep quiet about them. But neither religion nor politics should be excluded from the family dialogue. Questions about God are inevitable in our culture and, if history is any teacher, in any human society.

This doesn't mean that all fathers feel comfortable talking about God or their personal beliefs and practices in relationship to that entity. Once the conversation moves from abstract questions about God's existence and the possibility of heaven and hell to the more relational questions of prayer and spirituality, many dads are tempted to clam up. Typically, women have been perceived as the "more spiritual" half of the parenting team. And there is some evidence to back this up. It's a fact that in all of the major religious traditions—including Protestant, Catholic, and Jewish—women dominate the membership both in numbers and active participation. But facts and spiritual obligations are two different things. A father plays as important a role in the religious understanding of his children as a mother does. And both have a more lasting influence than any clergy.

To the extent that you are religious, let your children see it and understand it. If you pray or read Scripture, don't be afraid to lead your children in prayers or Scripture readings, as well. If you believe in a personal relationship with God, don't be embarrassed to describe that relationship to your children, or to confess your own sense of dependence and need.

Not all dads are religious in the traditional sense of the term. Some are agnostic, others atheist, and still others secular humanists. In a culture such as that which exists in the U.S., you may feel ambiguous or repressed and unwilling to share your religious feelings or beliefs with your children. You may feel even more so if Mom is the more traditionally religious of the two parents and is determined to provide some religious education for the children. But secular humanism is a spiritual perspective, too—one that is ethically grounded, highly emotional, and transforming. In fact, a case can be made for any ultimate allegiance being a "religion," whether it includes a supernatural being or not. Like all religions, humanism provides an ultimate moral framework in which to live, make decisions, and shape a mindset. Whatever framework you have chosen to build your life on, you can and should share it with your children.

Don't hide your spiritual side from your kids or discourage their curiosity or participation. Invite them to share their thoughts and their spirituality. In the end, you may both have a lot to teach each other.

88.

Draw the Line and Hold It

To a human observer, a goldfish in a bowl seems painfully confined. It swims and eats within the cubic foot or so that constitutes its entire "universe." We like to think that we're different; that our universe knows no limits and our freedom is without qualifiers.

Certainly, we don't live within the extreme confinement of the goldfish under normal circumstances. Yet we do live in a universe of boundaries. We have bodies that limit our ability to be in more than one place at one time. We deal with a mortality that limits the length of our lives. We have income and time restraints that limit our ability to engage in this or that activity. We have talent boundaries that limit what we can do professionally. The fact is that we're constrained by a variety of factors. Our bowl may be larger than the goldfish's, but it's still a bowl. And learning to live in that bowl—the universe, the planet, a nation, a community, or a home—is an important part of growing up.

Recognizing limitations is a large part of what life is all about. From their earliest years, children need boundaries. Without them, they would perish. Toddlers need to learn that fires and electric switches are out of bounds. Adolescents need to know that driving while drinking is out of bounds. If such boundaries are ignored, the consequences are literally life and death.

Beyond the obvious life and death boundaries that all responsible parents impose are less global boundaries that are unique and variable from one family to another. Yours are almost certainly different from those of your next-door neighbor, and you can be sure that your kids will let you know that, if it suits their interests. In fact, it matters less who is right and who is wrong about where to draw the line for kids than that each hold the line they've drawn. Don't get bent out of shape over the possibility that the boundaries you've established might be too restrictive or too broad. The point is that you put them in place and enforce them. Issues of safety and appropriate behavior aside, your children need to learn how to live within constraints imposed by others.

Make the rules clear and unambiguous. Repeat them often. And do not compromise, no matter how great the pressure from your children or your children's friends and parents. You do your children a great favor by sticking to the parameters that you've chosen. Your kids don't know or admit it, but far worse than overly narrow boundaries are constantly shifting boundaries. Shifting boundaries don't provide solid ground on which to stand. They do not communicate love or security. When you bend the rules under pressure (as opposed to when you realize that it is time to change because of your kids' maturing), you defeat the very goals that brought you to set limits in the first place. Don't get worked up over whether your rules are perfect. Be thoughtful about where you draw the line, and then hold it.

89.

Respect Their Mother

"Respect" is a small word that carries a large meaning. Respect sometimes means treating someone politely and courteously, even when you don't respect their judgment or decision-making in a particular situation. It also means treating someone in accord with their position or station, despite the fact that you don't think much of the job that they're doing. Respect for your partner and your relationship needs to transcend particular issues over child-rearing in all but extreme situations. Parents who want their home and family to thrive learn how to rise above friction and treat one another with respect.

That can be easier said than done. After a day at work, when nothing seems to have gone right, you can come home to a household that pushes the limits of your patience and judgment. Your child has refused to clean a messy room and has told his mom that the room will not be cleaned anytime soon. It is, after all, "my room," he declares. Mom responds by saying, "That's fine, but you're grounded; you will stay in your room and not go out until it's clean. Take as long as you like." You encounter your child at the door as you walk in. "Mom won't let me go out over a silly rule, and now I can't play soccer. I'll be thrown off the team!"

At this point, you may want to say, "Okay, play soccer now, and we'll deal with the room later." The trouble is that the kid's mom has already laid down the law. By refusing to back her up, you have diminished her authority, and perhaps even her self-confidence and self-respect. Meanwhile, your child has emerged with an artificially expanded sense of self-confidence and the lesson learned that disobeying Mom works if Dad can be enlisted as an ally, or can even just be made to stay neutral.

If it's true that sometimes children encourage (or even incite) parents to disagree and divide, it's also true that children sometimes rebel against one parent and expect the other to "butt out" of a "fair fight." This, too, misses the point of hierarchy in the family and partnership in parenting. Rebellion in children is a part of the natural order of growing up, and should not be cause for undue alarm. But rebels, with or without a cause, require a united front. Even if you think that the kids' mother may have overreacted, loyalty and respect demand that you publicly side with her.

Respect for Mom is appropriate, and symbolizes respect for the entire entity of the nuclear family and the necessary hierarchy that frames it. Families start, after all, with parents in intimate partnership, producing offspring, and exercising love and control over it. The family develops into a loving entity of adults in charge of maturing children that will endure until the day that the kids become self-sustaining adults. Give Mom the respect that her role deserves. If you must disagree about rules of child-rearing, duke it out in private.

90.

Give Grandparents Their Due

In most American households today, the nuclear family of parents and children, or the "single-parent" family, is most common. In times past, as many as three generations often lived under one roof; or if they no longer shared one roof, they lived side by side on one farm or in one town. Today, hundreds or even thousands of miles may separate grandparents from their children and grandchildren, and the oldest generation may be contributing nothing to the economic well-being of the nuclear family. But they are still around, and they can count enormously in your children's lives.

You can bridge the gap between your parents and your children in a way that helps the kids understand that you, too, were once a child, who grew up under the authority of the people they know as grandparents. In time, you grew up to become the adult equal of your parents, just as your children will. But even in your equality, you have respect for the people who raised you. They will always be your elders, and they deserve honor and a vital relationship with their descendants.

Meanwhile, grandparents can offer a lot to their grandchildren. Here, you can serve as a facilitator, encouraging relationships and letting them evolve on their own terms. Because grandparents typically have no immediate responsibility for their grandchildren, and because they often have more discretionary time and money than they did in their family years, they can do things with or for their grandchildren that they couldn't do for their own children. You may be tempted to resent the special treatment that you never received. Or you may feel that your upbringing was on the mark, and the grandfolks are now spoiling the next generation, or even undermining your relationship with your children. In most cases, this is wrongheaded. Children intuitively distinguish grandparents from parents, and parents do, in fact, rule.

Grandparents won't be around forever. By making room for them in the life of your family, you promote a "living history" for yourself and your children that will last beyond your parents' immediate lives. Your children will grow up with a multigenerational perspective that they, in turn, will bring to their child-rearing years a shockingly short time in the future. It balances immediate concerns with the developments and changes over a lifetime, allowing new parents to glimpse the larger picture with some peace and humor. Give grandparents their due without fussing over perennial quirks or your own insecurities. It's a gift from you to the next generation and to yourself.

91.

Honor Memories

Memories are some of the most precious possessions we acquire in our life's journeys. An oldie but goodie can bring us to a moment in our youth as if it were yesterday. A saved love letter from the seventh grade stands as a poignant marker of "puppy love."

As a wise adult, you can help to preserve memories in the lives of your children by being attuned to important events and documenting them for the future. In this age of camcorders, digital cameras, and electronic texts, there's no shortage of technological aids. But one thing is as clear now as in the prior generation: Technology can help preserve memories enormously, but it can't do it all.

Growing up is filled with moments in time that don't need a brilliant sunset or a mountaintop view to make them worthy of recording. To the outward eye, they can be quite ordinary, but to the intimate eye of love, something unforgettable is happening. Perhaps it's a trip that you make with your child; or maybe it's a long walk; or it may be a peak experience in achievement, revelation, or relationship.

By making and preserving a record, you say: "Hold this in your memory, youngster; it's precious and something that you'll never experience again."

See through your children's eyes as you learn to know and understand them. Add to that your own understanding of what lives on in a person's memory. Make a point of providing access to the tools of remembrance. In honoring their memories, you not only gift your children with the past, you signal your appreciation of the lives that they are building.

92.

Share Your Heritage

As parents, we have the privilege of raising our children with an understanding of the commonalties that make us varied citizens of a single nation. Our tensile strength as a nation and our sense of unity derive from cultural and legal acceptance of all groups as equally and authentically "American." It is important that our children understand rule by constitutional law. It is important that they understand individualism and the inalienable rights of all individuals above any claims of larger entities such as governments, political parties, churches, or armies. And it is important that they understand the competitive free markets and the economic equal opportunity of the society they will inhabit.

But alongside these commonalties, we can also encourage our children to respect and appreciate the distinctive aspects of their individual family heritages. Part of heritage is history: the family genealogy as far back as you can trace it. Many schools direct their students to look at family histories, and you would be well-advised to participate in these explorations and share the pride that comes with them.

Family histories often meld into larger histories of ethnic, racial, or religious subgroups in American history. These, too, are worth discovering, recounting, and remembering. Much as your children may dislike "history" in the academic sense, they will discover a genuine interest when it comes to their own history. "What did my great-grandparents do when they arrived in this country?" "Did any of my ancestors fight in World War I?" "Why do we live in this part of the country?" These questions frequently lead to other questions, and the more you know, the more the conversation will grow.

Of course, not everyone has a happy family history, and you may find it too difficult to talk about some ancestors. But there is probably some point of pride that you can find in your past or in the history of your ethnic group that can be celebrated without delving into unhappy personal experiences. In the process, you can give your children an investment in that. In times of personal stress and uncertainty, such a sense of a larger connection can be an immense source of security.

Whether you wish to identify yourself as, say, Italian-American, African-American, Protestant, Catholic, or Jew is an individual choice. But at some level, you own and can find a heritage. In the final analysis, as you share your heritage with your children, you invest in their destiny.

93.

Love the Day
That They Were Born

Why are birthdays so important? Birthdays are the only personalized and individual markers that recur annually in our lives; they deserve to be treated as special holidays in the lives of our children. Every person is born on a specific date on the calendar, and comes of age in significant religious and political ways on specific dates (thirteen for a bar or bat mitzvah, sixteen for driving, eighteen for voting, twenty-one for drinking, fifty-five for early retirement). One way we track the progress of our lives is the observance and celebration of our birth dates.

How can you help make your children's birthdays special? For starters, be involved. While it's unrealistic to think that you or Mom can take a day off from work or that the birthday child will be exempted from school, the day deserves to be filled with memory-making. Weekends close to birthdays are also wonderful opportunities to bring in friends, extended family, and neighbors, if only for a birthday cake and an energetic round of "Happy Birthday to You."

While all birthdays deserve your special time and attention, some may carry more importance than others. "Sweet sixteen" birthdays for daughters may be an occasion for a special one-on-one. This is the age when tradition says that girls begin to become women—the age when they get serious about dating and young men occupy an important space in their lives. You can signal the transition that is taking place by taking your daughter out for a father-daughter "date" and treating her as the young woman she is becoming.

Probably the greatest present a boy receives comes at age sixteen, too, but it has little to do with moms and dads and parties. A driver's license gives imagined freedom of unprecedented scope. For many families, there is no special sixteenth birthday for sons quite like that for daughters. However, you can be sensitive to whatever year may express a similar time of symbolic transition from childhood to the beginning of young manhood for your boys. Perhaps you have a family tradition of a fishing or hunting trip at age fourteen, fifteen, or sixteen. Perhaps it's an outing with Dad and Granddad. These provide marvelous opportunities for boys to know and experience their grandfathers as men. Such experiences become a benchmark that will never be forgotten.

As your children become adults, you need to continue to remember birthdays. At some profound level, the child in us never disappears, and even a forty-year-old will appreciate a birthday card from a parent. Don't let the mailing of birthday cards and the sentiments that they contain be defined as "women's stuff." Add your touch to a card, even if it's only a sentence penned at the bottom. What's important to your children at any age is that you remember the magical day they were born with gratitude and love.

94.

Take a Hike

Some families are born jocks. Parents play tennis, ski, and join softball leagues or golf clubs, while children fill all sports seasons with team activities that keep them fit and active. In many ways, such families epitomize the "all-American family" featured on cereal boxes and TV sitcoms.

But dads who are not scratch golfers and children who are not sports-stars-to-be need not sweat it. Athletic prowess is something quite separate from physical fitness and body awareness. Athleticism comes as a particular gift, and often goes with age; fitness and positive body awareness are lifelong traits that you can cultivate in yourself and your children.

Families need to include physical activity as part of their time together. Swimming outings, nature walks, and bike trips offer wonderful opportunities for physical activity that can be done as a family without any great talent for sports. State parks surround every community and afford beautiful trails that a family can hike with virtually no expense and a reasonable time commitment. A regularly scheduled Saturday or Sunday morning outing can become a cherished family tradition that continues even when adult children come home for visits.

Families need not exercise together all of the time to promote a common pursuit of physical fitness. The best exercise is sustainable for a lifetime, and should be as regular as body hygiene or eating a meal. No one can thrive without it. By actively exercising your own body, you model a lifetime pursuit that children will naturally emulate.

The mental aspect of physical activity cannot be minimized. Even though few of us have the body of a highly trained Olympian, exercise changes everyone's body. Muscles that were soft and flabby can be made hard and serviceable. Lungs that gasp after a hundred-yard jog can build up to miles. And legs that can pedal a bike no more than five minutes can extend that duration to hours. If you take pride in physical progress and become more aware of your physical condition, you'll easily instill that sense of pride and accomplishment in your children. Whether exercising with them or apart, take note of their fitness and praise signs of progress.

If progress lapses at times, don't make a big deal out of it. Guilt trips for fitness don't work—they can even boomerang. You have the opportunity to make your children feel "at home" with their bodies and feel good about them. When progress is slow, praise your kids for their efforts. Value each child's physical being for what it is.

About the time that adolescence arrives, you may see your children dispense with the physical routines of earlier years.

Sometimes it's rebellion against doing what you do, including exercise. Sometimes it's disappointment or frustrated relationships that lead to abusive eating or drug abuses. While you don't want to overreact, you also don't want to be naive. Love for your children and acceptance of who they are and how they're made does not mean tolerating abuse. You can't always accept their explanations for body (or mood) changes at face value. When things don't seem right, trust your instincts and be a skeptic. If you are alert and observant, you will notice changes that need to be actively pursued.

Within the realm of normal adolescent behavior, however, the good habits of body and mind that you encourage will stick. Your kids may lay off for a time, but they're likely to return to what you've shown them over the long haul.

95.

Cook Together

Okay, so you're not a cook. There is no time that bonds a father to his family more than mealtime. It's a time when you actually see everyone in one place, face them across a table, or chow down in front of a good video that you can talk about later. But it can also be a time when you embark on a small-size family project with a product for your efforts that everyone can enjoy.

Cooking together doesn't have to mean a four-course gourmet meal. It doesn't even have to mean a meal in any conventional sense. How about conspiring on a big batch of designer popcorn, with every family member choosing a different topping? Or make a simple meal that takes a lot of different small jobs to prepare, such as tacos. Everybody enters into the process and eats the bounty as a proud team.

Perhaps you have one meal that you consider your specialty. Lots of dads major in weekend breakfasts, with pancakes, waffles, or bacon and eggs. Some dads are kings of the barbecue. If that's your domain, consider pulling the kids into it with you. Aside from the learning experience for them, there's the pleasure of spending time together with a common goal as your focus. Such occasions forge bonds and build memories that you'll never orchestrate directly.

Of course, you may be one of that growing breed, the dad who is the family's primary cook. If that's you, you don't need any advice on how to make sous-chefs out of your kids. You may not even need the suggestion. If you haven't thought of getting them involved, however, think of it now.

The upshot of all of this is that the more you can make the whole family co-participants in meals, the closer your family will grow. Include the kids in setup, preparation, cooking, and cleanup. Dads who don't cook can always clean—in fact, they can help clean even if they *do* cook. And it can be an extra courtesy on the nights that Mom handles all of the food preparation for the rest of the gang to tell her to step aside and relax while they handle all the cleaning. One suggestion: If you do clean up together, try avoiding the dishwasher once in a while, and wash and dry the plates yourselves. These are mindless exercises, and the time spent doing them will be filled with one-on-one conversation.

The time will come when daily mealtimes are not an option anymore for you and your kids. There's no time like the present to turn what is sometimes considered a chore—preparing, serving, and cleaning up after a meal—into a source of fun, togetherness, and pride of accomplishment.

96.

Be a Window to the World

No matter how circumscribed our lives might be by jobs, location, routines, or responsibilities, we owe it to ourselves and our children to build a bigger, broader range of vision than what is right before our eyes. For many, many years, kids have a perspective that depends primarily on what their home and school offer. Sometimes these venues offer a way of seeing that is ripe with ideas, options, and viewpoints. More often, consensus rules in these environments. We have a family culture and a regional culture that give us a certain slant and fixed ideas about what is and what might be in the future.

Don't be trapped by where you are or what is habitual, either in attitude, behavior, or activity. Instead, open yourself to the rewarding and thrilling pastime of seeking out other ways of seeing and thinking, other cultural norms, and other possible future directions. Subscribe to media that espouse views that differ from your own. Read authors that you've never read. Go on field trips. Take advantage of cultural events outside of your own region. Plan a trip to a foreign country. Make sure to include your children in all of this.

Have you ever gone window shopping? As you look in all of the windows showcasing their wares, you discover new possibilities that suggest places and pastimes that haven't yet been yours. That is precisely the state of mind you want to cultivate in your children. Encourage them to open new windows on the world and see new visions. There is no reason why every child can't be a sort of "visionary."

Whether you bring ideas into your home or venture out in search of them, you can encourage the visionary in your kids by stimulating imagination with questions. Play the "what if?" game with abandon: "What if we could be invisible and go wherever we wanted unseen? Where would you like to go?" "What if we could go back in a time machine to any time or place we wanted?" Questions like these are fun for everyone, and serve to lift people out of the here and now into the world of unrealized possibilities.

Don't discourage your children from daydreaming. Flights of imagination can carry them far away. Daydreams are natural, and are the stuff of which creativity and strong coping mechanisms are made. Let their souls take flight alongside their minds and imaginations.

Life can become tedious when all you see are the four walls around you or the unchanging faces in your hometown. It is the same for your children. Be one of their windows onto a bigger world, and you'll exchange the ho-hum for a thrilling sense of what's waiting "out there."

97.

Rise to the Occasion

One of the greatest opportunities that a dad receives is in a genuine cry for help from his child. All kids face moments of desperation and dread in their lives. Sometimes they get into trouble with authorities and want to hide it from the family. Sometimes it's fear in the face of a failure that nobody else in the family experienced. Sometimes it's simply a fear of things that go bump in the night. Who can they turn to for help? If you're always busy and preoccupied with your own life and work, chances are that it won't be you. Either your children will turn to some other significant person in their lives, or, failing that, will turn to escapes such as drugs or unacceptable behavior.

When your child asks for help, view that moment as a special gift, not an obligation or an unwanted distraction from your immediate preoccupation. Don't turn away. Don't postpone. It's the chance to hold your child's heart and soul, troubles and fears, in the palm of your hand. It's a rare and wonderful moment, and it can lead to a bond that will last a lifetime.

Pleas for help start at birth, and Mom is a prominent presence out of biological necessity. If you make yourself part of the answer from infancy on, you will begin a pattern. In later years, your children will turn naturally to you and say: "Dad, can you help me?" If you're starting late on the scene as a helper, don't let that stop you. Late is better than never, and may even be just in time.

98.

Build a Friendship

If you could sketch an ideal relationship with your children when they become adults and parents themselves, what would it look like? It's worth it to explore this exercise often, for it will shape the way that you interact with your children as they grow up. We become so immersed in our kids as children that we can forget that this is not a permanent state. All of the innocence, ignorance, naivete, and rebellion will not last forever. Our children will move closer and closer to becoming our peers.

At least, that's the way it should be. Some parents, to be sure, try to capture their children as children forever. They can't face the fact that what had defined their world and station for decades is changing radically as their children come of age. Such a perspective can become destructive: It almost certainly either arrests the development of the children, or ruptures the relationship between adult children and adult parents—or both. Children do grow up, and what they need from you when they do is a dad who has the vision to make the transition.

If pressed, most dads would choose for their adult children to be their friends. Friends care about each other and look out for each other. Friends like one another and enjoy being in one another's presence. Of course, you will love your children forever. But will you like them and enjoy being in their presence as fellow adults? And will they like *you*?

Not surprisingly, the makings of friendship begin in your children's early years. Without ever forgetting the privileges and responsibilities of rank, you can let your humanity show. Share the dreams that your children are old enough to understand. Express your fears, insofar as they don't undermine your children's sense of security or surpass their comprehension. Knowing that parents have dreams and fears of their own will not scar your children for life. It will simply allow them to know you better.

There comes a time in a dad's life when he realizes that his son is stronger, faster, and more flexible than he is. In like manner, he'll face the time when his daughter is her own woman, independent, possibly tied to another man, and even a mother in her own right. Gradually, the roles will change as the stronger become weaker and the children become parents. These times can be wonderful—or unbearably trying and disillusioning. It all depends on the nature of the relationship. If your sons and daughters are also your friends, their ascent to adulthood will be a joy. If they're estranged, the loneliness will be painful.

The point of effective parenting is to imagine this evolution before your children are capable of seeing it for themselves. Your job includes preparing them for their adulthood. In the process, you will save yourself needless suffering and alienation if you prepare yourself, as well. Even as you parent your dependent children, look beyond them to the adult friends they have the potential to become. Who knows? They may even become the best friends you'll ever have.

99.

Celebrate Success

Most dads don't think of themselves as cheerleaders. Captains, cleanup hitters, or quarterbacks, yes—but generally not cheerleaders. Yet in your family, cheerleading is often exactly what's called for when the time comes to celebrate your children's successes and milestones, or to keep them going when their nerve or energy fails. Cheerleading is more than being a fan. It's being the backup battery, fueling the forward momentum, and yelling, "Hooray!" at the finish line, all wrapped up in one.

Some dads give praise more easily than others do. Some dads don't require a lot of praise themselves to be confident and self-assured. They know that they do a good job and they know that their family knows. It doesn't occur to them to dish it out. But most kids have an unending need and desire for feedback, especially of the positive sort. They move forward with constant glances over their shoulders to make sure that you're watching. And they wait for your praise when they've earned it.

By celebrating your kids' efforts and achievements, you become part of the action. At some deep level, you're not simply reflecting your children's activity; you're helping to shape it. By continuing to cheer them on, you help to build their resolve and confidence. This is the meaning of "home court advantage." Your cheerleading gives your kids their own home court advantage.

Graduations, parts in school plays, music recitals, honor rolls, first jobs, and new skills—are all milestone achievements in your children's lives that will never be replicated. Don't hold out for even greater successes down the road that will really engage your pride and celebration. They may never come. From the earliest years, take every day and every accomplishment as an occasion to cheer as if your child had just won the World Series.

100.

Have Fun

Fathers are under a lot of pressure to "know best." They are simultaneously caregivers, providers, role models, and when necessary, disciplinarians. These are serious roles, to be sure. But don't ever take yourself so seriously that you can't laugh at your role as Dad and keep a light touch. It's a fact that father doesn't "know best" all of the time, and will make mistakes along the way. Don't stress over the mistakes and missteps so much that you can no longer have fun during the precious few years that you're raising kids. Life is a gift, and life with children—despite the work and worry that attend it—is a gift multiplied with grace notes. As you keep on keeping on in your role as Dad, remember to savor the moments and enjoy the ride.